Freddie Mercury

An Intimate Biography

David Bret

A catalogue record for this book is available from the British
Library.

ISBN: 978-1-291-81108-7

This book is dedicated to Elizabeth Taylor, with grateful thanks
from her "loveable little shit".....

N'oubliez pas...La vie sans amis c'est comme un jardin sans
fleurs

Freddie Mercury

An Intimate Biography

David Bret

Acknowledgements

Writing this book would not have been possible had it not been for the inspiration, criticism and love of that select group of individuals whom I will always regard as my true family and *autre coeur*: Barbara, Marlene Dietrich, Dorothy Squires, Roger Normand, Irene Bevan, René Chevalier, Axel Dotti—*que vous dormez en paix*. Jacqueline Danno, Betty & Gérard Gamain, Annick Roux, Terry Sanderson, John & Ann Taylor. For sharing her private thoughts and reminiscences with me, but more so for being such a wonderful friend to Freddie, my heart goes out to **Montserrat Caballé**. No man could have wished for a more understanding confidante. I am also indebted to Isabelle Caballé, David Evans, Jim Jenkins, Kurt, Michael, Mike Moran, Elaine Paige, Kate Weston and David Wigg. Not forgetting David Bolt, my agent Guy Rose, and his lovely wife, Alex. Also Jacky Gunn and Val Moss of The International Queen Fan Club, Hannie Roggeveden of The Official Dutch Queen Fan Club, Frieda Sarhadi of *The Royal Gazette*....and **Saint Elizabeth Taylor**.

For their help and contribution to this book I also thank the following: Mary Austin, Jason Barker, Iain Blair, Rusi Dalal, Andy Davis, Adrian Deevoy, Robin Denselow, Harry Doherty, Richard Ellis, David Evans, Sharon Feinstein, John Gill, David Hancock, Tony Hicks, Bill Higgins, Jim Hutton, James Johnson, Henrietta Knight, Gotz Kuhnemund, Alain Lavanne, John Marshall, Geoff Mayfield, Richard Middleton, Kate Molly, Chris Morris, Jeff Moses, Mike Parker, Tony Parsons, Willie Pepper, Mark Putterford, David Quantick, Julianne Regan, Robert Sandall, Paul Scott, Jonathan Singer, Merrill Shindler, Richard Smith, Peter Stein, Tony Stewart, Andy Stout, Sally Stratton, Baudouin Struye, Phil Sutcliffe, Johnny Waller, Stephen Williams, Anthony Wood, Toby Young, the Principal (1995) of St Peter's School, Panchgani.

4

Thanks also to the following publications past and present:
The Baghdad Observer, Billboard, Daily Express, Daily Mirror, Daily Telegraph, Dayton Daily News, Gay Times, Guitarist, The Guardian, Hard-Rock Francais, Kerrang, London Evening Standard, London Press Service, Metal Hammer, More-Belgique, Music Express, Music & Media, New Musical Express, News of the World, New York Globe, OK, Oxford Mail, People, Playgirl, Q, Record Collector, Record & Popswop Mirror, Rock-Circus, Rockline, RIP, RSVP, Sounds, Sun, Sunday Mirror, Sunday Times, Time Out, Today, Tracks, The Times, Top 40.
Most of all, a big, BIG thankyou to Freddie, for being there....and to my wife Jeanne who is still the keeper of my soul.

Foreword by Montserrat Caballé

Throughout Europe, and in America and Japan, wherever I sing I am still approached by Freddie Mercury's fans. They ask me what he was like to work with. They tell me how much they love him still, that when he died, part of them died with him.

Freddie's music and his qualities as a human being directly touched the hearts of his admirers, yet he is constantly criticized and his life turned into a moral epic. No one person has the right to judge another person. Freddie lived his life without pretence, exactly the way he felt he should, and he should be respected for that. Even those finest examples of humanity—Gandhi and Mother Theresa of Calcutta—admitted that they had faults, and if they considered themselves imperfect in any way, who are we to judge a man who brought so much joy and goodness to the world?

I find it very moving to witness such devotion, yet I am not surprised because Freddie was a good, non-violent, peace-loving man who was generous not just to his friends and those he loved, but to others who suffered the way he did.

I will always remember Freddie as a good friend, an honest and courageous man—especially towards the end of his life—a man who was very, very special for thousands of people. And you know, thousands of people cannot be wrong.

Montserrat Caballé, Barcelona, August 1996

Introduction

> You can have everything in the world and still be the
> loneliest man—that is the most bitter type of loneliness.
> Success has brought me world idolization and millions of
> pounds, but it's prevented me from having the one thing
> we all need—a loving, on-going relationship.

This was Freddie Mercury—pop icon, showman, raconteur, diva,
authority on the human condition, clown-prince, unquestionable
genius—speaking in a rare interview with the *News of the World*
in April 1985. The occasion commemorated the release of his
album, *Mr Bad Guy*, comprising eleven self-composed songs,
several of which may retrospectively be regarded as portentous:
'There Must Be More To Life Than This', 'Love Me Like There's
No Tomorrow', 'My Love Is Dangerous', 'Fooling Around'....

Friends and colleagues have readily maintained that Freddie's
promiscuity—no different from that of the average pop star,
regardless of sexual preference—was precipitated and fuelled by
an abject loneliness stemming from a fragmented childhood
which, though never lacking in love and affection, had seen him
endure lengthy periods of separation from his family. 'My biggest
nightmare has always been walking into an empty bedroom,' he
admitted once, in a statement reminiscent of those final, torturous
Judy Garland concerts in London when she had screamed, 'I don't
wanna go home! What is there at home for me?' It was this
crippling loneliness which prompted Freddie to say, after
performing in front of 250,000 wildly adoring fans in Rio de
Janeiro, 'I was the loneliest person there.'

Freddie's psyche may be readily associated with that of those
monstres sacrées, mostly female, who become so embroiled in
their public personae—married to their audiences—that any kind

of relationship, physical or otherwise, cannot be easily sustained while the legend persists. Yet persist it must, otherwise existence would be meaningless. The list is endless: Bette Davis, Joan Crawford, Rock Hudson, Edith Piaf, Tallulah Bankhead, Marlene Dietrich, Greta Garbo—all greatly admired by Freddie Mercury, all searching for that crock of gold at the end of the rainbow, but only coming close to finding it in the glare of the spotlight.

Like these *alter egos*, Freddie is to be commended for his honesty. When asked if he was homosexual, James Dean had quipped, 'Well, I'm certainly not going through life with one hand tied behind my back!' Freddie's response to the same question, posed by a journalist from the *New Musical Express*, was, 'I've had more lovers than Elizabeth Taylor. I've got a big bed which sleeps six. I'm as gay as a daffodil, my dear!' This was Freddie at his most flippant—the newspapers expected an outrageous reply and were never disappointed. A few years later, one could only detect the note of anguish in his voice when he confessed that love, for him, was like playing Russian roulette. He added, 'I try to hold back when I'm attracted to someone, but I just can't control love. It runs riot. All my one-night stands are just me playing my part.'

This was Freddie's essence, a Janus character who was equally at home telling the media that he was 'essentially a private man', never becoming a spokesman for the gay community, hardly ever expressing his views on contentious issues. On the other side of the coin, however, he was blatantly extroverted, rebellious, more outrageous than *any* of his contemporaries, and one of the most thrilling personalities of the last half of the twentieth century.

He was probably best summed up by John Marshall of *Gay Times*—whose lengthy, uncompromising eulogy in January 1992 served as a welcome antidote to the wealth of often pretentious and sometimes downright poisonous obituaries which had appeared in the British press:

He was a 'scene-queen', not afraid to publicly express his gayness, and unwilling to analyse or justify his lifestyle. It was as if Freddie was saying to the world, 'I am what I am. So what?' And that in itself was a statement.

Mad about the boy! (Redferns)

One: I Can HearMusic!

He was born Faroukh Bulsara, at the Government Hospital on the small island of Zanzibar, off the coast of what was then Tanganyika, on 5 September 1946—the eldest child of Bomi, an itinerant Persian clerk with the British government who with his wife Jer had set up home in Zanzibar, after leaving their native Bombay. The Bulsaras were Parsees—followers of Zoroaster, and direct descendants of those Persians who had fled to India in the seventh and eighth centuries to avoid Muslim persecution. They were not an inordinately wealthy family by any means though, in common with most colonials in the last years of the Raj, the Bulsaras did have a coterie of low-paid but loyal servants which catered for their every need—though there was *never* anyone there to fasten his shoelaces for him and wash his neck, as Freddie once joked.

When he was five, Faroukh enrolled at the local missionary school. Soon afterwards, in 1952, his only sister, Kashmira, was born. Then, in 1954, Bomi was transferred back to Bombay, still in the same employ, but with a larger 'round' of high courts to visit. So that his education would not suffer—he was an alert, intelligent child—Bomi had his son enrolled at St Peter's, a prestigious English boarding school at Panchgani, a hill-station some fifty miles from Bombay. The move coincided with Faroukh being ordained a fully-fledged Parsee, partaking of the *Navjote*, or cleansing ritual, and reciting the sacred prayers of Zoroaster while donning the *sudreh* or traditional white muslin shirt of purity.

Faroukh had never been really close to his father, largely on account of Bomi's lengthy absences from home. Now, in an utterly Etonesque environment, the Faroukh was rapidly dispensed with. For the rest of his life he would be known only as

Freddie, or by intimate friends such as Elton John, as Melina after the famous Greek actress, Melina Mercouri, who told me herself some years later that some of *her* close friend had called her Freddie! He also adapted readily to the school's Spartan discipline, reflecting, 'You *had* to do as you were told, so the most sensible thing was to make the best of it. I learned how to look after myself, and I grew up very quickly.'

In keeping with colonial tradition, St Peter's School followed a typically 'gung-ho' sporting calendar: rugby, cricket, football, boxing, table tennis and athletics. Freddie loathed cricket and most track events—according to one school pal, 'He would scurry down the track like a demented Jerry Lewis.' With equal fervour, he enjoyed boxing and table tennis, becoming school champion by the age of ten. In later years there would often be a table in the corner of the recording studio, and to give his opponent a chance against his exceptional skills he would always play left-handed, with the other hand behind his back.

Freddie was also efficient at English, though his true forte was art, a medium which nevertheless found him at his most frenetic. Friends have testified that in these early days, though the enthusiasm and talent were undoubtedly there, patience was not one of Freddie's finer virtues and he hardly ever completed a picture or drawing. Like many boys, he collected postage stamps. The collection he amassed was not particularly large, but it did contain many early items from Zanzibar: many years later his 'Blue Album' would be sold for thousands of pounds and the proceeds donated to charity.

Another important element in Freddie's development was his interest in music, particularly in the recordings of Lata Mangeshkar, India's top entertainer. Born in 1929 and known as 'The Nightingale of India', this fascinating performer had been the favourite of the country's first Prime Minister, Pandit Nehru. She performed in twenty languages including Sanskrit and Hindi, and had a vast repertoire of 30,000 songs. The very first concert Freddie attended, in November 1959, was a gala performance by Mangeshkar in Bombay. The sheer power of her voice and her range of material so fascinated him that he saw her again in Poona, and in Panchgani in 1961, when she paid a visit to St Peter's to sing at their summer fete. Mangeshkar and several others have since maintained that Freddie Mercury would have made a fine playback singer, though with his vibrant personality and love of showing off, it is doubtful that he would have ever been satisfied to limit himself to mere film soundtracks and not being seen.

The library at St Peter's housed an extensive collection of Lata Mangeshkar records, many albums by the equally legendary Egyptian singer Oum Kalthoum (1904-75), whom Freddie also frequently impersonated, and a good many more be-bop, twist, Cliff Richard and Tommy Steele records sent over from England. He played anything he could get his hands on—all were instrumental in forging his future. Amateur dramatics, too, were an important part of Freddie's curriculum, and because it was an all-male environment, St Peter's had long-since adopted Shakespeare's own tradition that the female roles be played by boys. Freddie considered that this was going a little *too* far, though from his early teens he was well aware of the 'camp' aspect of dramatization because of his admiration of Gielgud and Olivier, whose over-the-top film portrayals of the bard's heroes and villains were shown regularly at the school. Like all public schools, too, St Peter's had its clandestine coterie of homosexuals with whom Freddie felt perfectly comfortable once he became aware of his own sexuality—mindless of the fact that sex outside marriage, let alone with a member of one's own gender, was fiercely condemned by the Parsee religion.

Freddie's first love affair, if it can be deemed such, occurred during the Spring of 1961 when he was fourteen, with a 17-year-old youth nicknamed 'The Master' on account of his snooty Noel Coward mannerisms. 'I had a crush on The Master, and would have done *anything* for him,' Freddie confessed. 'Going to bed with him didn't feel wrong, and though I'd never made love with a woman, I asked myself if *that* would be worth all the fuss!"

There was much more to it than this. The Master—his name was Robert—was an overweight, unattractive, reprehensible individual who took advantage of Freddie's slight physique and timidity by bullying him into having sex with him. One of Freddie's classmates (still living in Panchgani when interviewed in 1995) who may only be identified as Michael, recounted Freddie's account of how he lost his virginity to this young man:

> Several of Freddie's pals, myself included, knew that we were gay from quite early on, but we were terrified to do anything about it. The consequences of being caught out those days were horrendous, so instead of actually doing anything, we would get our kicks from spying on the older boys while they were bathing. Unfortunately, Freddie was nabbed by The Master and carted off to the gardener's shed where he was knocked about a bit and forced to have sex with him. Freddie told me about it a couple of weeks later, but when I asked him why he hadn't reported the matter to the Principal, he said that it was because he'd enjoyed the experience so much. Later, of course, he told me that he'd only stuck with The Master because he'd been petrified of admitting his feelings to anyone else in case he ended up being sent down. What also struck me as strange, certainly at that time, was the fact that on account of The Master, poor Freddie assumed that S and M and homosexuality went hand in glove. Then, after the summer term The Master returned to England to live with his family—and Freddie

fell head-over-heels in love with a beautiful Indian boy who worked in the gardens. His name was Sanjay, he was twenty-three, and he and Freddie spent as much time together as they could, mostly at weekends, until Freddie left the school.

Meanwhile, encouraging him in his artistic interests, Freddie's father consented to an increase in his allowance so that he could take up a musical instrument. Freddie chose the piano, substituted Mangeshkar for Mozart, and within the space of a few years had passed his Grade IV Theory & Practical. He joined the school's choir, which though multicultural was compelled to perform traditional Christian hymns, Handel, Bach, and even Gregorian chants and Jewish *cheseds*. More importantly for Freddie, with a group of friends and despite his intense shyness, he formed his first band, the Hectics, which, though only allowed to perform at in-house functions, fared reasonably well.

Freddie, strange to say in view of his later exhibitionism, was not the Hectic's frontman—this honour went to a youngster named Bruce Murray. In 1962, however, this somewhat idyllic existence was brought to a halt when Freddie sat his 'O' levels. Achieving good results in English Language, History, Art and Music, he announced that he had had enough of school and a few weeks later—bidding his beloved Sanjay goodbye—he returned to his family in Zanzibar.

The island protectorate was about to enter a period of political turmoil as it battled towards Independence from the British. The first round of elections took place towards the end of 1963—when most experts expected the Africans who formed the majority of the population to win. They did not, succumbing to the Arab minority in this and the next two polls until, on 10 December 1963, Zanzibar broke free of British rule. One month later it emerged with Tanganyika to form Tanzania—causing the

Africans to mount an unsuccessful insurrection but one which forced the flight of thousands of Britons and Indians. The Bulsaras, cramming what belongings they could into a few suitcases, headed for England. For a while they stayed with relatives in Feltham, Middlesex, before purchasing a modest semi in the area. Bomi then took a job as an accountant with the Trust House Forté group, while Freddie enrolled on a course with Isleworth Polytechnic—it was essential that he gain his Art 'A' level to ensure a place at college. His parents were opposed to the idea. Like a great many colonials, they tended to frown upon the artistic milieu, and had probably hoped that Freddie might follow in his father's footsteps. Also, while the Bulsaras shunned the British society they had been forcibly ejected into, retreating into the tiny Parsee community, Freddie greedily lapped up his exciting new world of 'Swinging Sixties' London. For a time, according to Rusi Dalal, who had grown up with Freddie in Zanzibar, he would drop in at the Parsee Temple in West Hampstead, but as these visits decreased, he found himself more and more distanced from his family.

In his spare time and during the holidays, refusing to accept handouts from his parents, Freddie supported himself with a variety of *ad hoc* jobs. He washed pots in the kitchens at Heathrow airport, and stacked crates at a warehouse on the Feltham Industrial Estate. Here, he was ribbed by some of the rough-and-ready factory hands on account of his unusual colouring, protruding front teeth, posh accent and effeminate mannerisms, though he soon won everyone over with his ready charm and knack of self-parody. 'Nobody could take the piss out of me as much as I could take the piss out of myself,' he later said.

At the end of his college course, in April 1966, Freddie's hard work was rewarded with a Grade A pass in Art, and he was accepted for a course in graphic design by Ealing College of Art, whose former students included Peter Townshend, who had formed The Who there, and the Small Faces' Ronnie Wood, later of the Rolling Stones. Freddie's consuming passion whilst there was Jimi Hendrix, the hard-living, drug-addicted rock star from Seattle. He executed dozens of paintings and drawings of his idol, which he framed and hung on the walls of his flat. On occasions he aped Hendrix in class, ruffling his hair and strumming away on an imaginary guitar—a 12-inch ruler—while belting out 'Purple Haze'.

Freddie's closest friend at Ealing was Tim Staffell, already a pop 'veteran'. In 1964, with three fellow pupils from Hampton Grammar School, vocalist Staffell had formed the futuristic group 1984, which had been augmented by a Feltham guitarist named Brian May. Aided by his father, May had built his own soon-to-be-legendary 'Red Special' guitar, to his own specification for just £8 using bits and bobs from around the house—an antique fire-surround for the neck, and his mother's pearl buttons for the fret-markers. The group had split in 1967, though May and Staffell—the former enrolling on an Astro-physics course at Imperial College—remained close and quickly set about forming another group. May placed an advertisement on his college noticeboard: 'Wanted: Ginger Baker-Type Drummer'.

The pair settled on Roger Taylor, an 18-year-old dentistry student, Norfolk-born, but for many years a resident of Truro, in Cornwall. The group was Smile, which in 28 October made a prestigious début at Imperial College supporting Pink Floyd. As a matter of course, Tim Staffell introduced Freddie to the band, and Brian May was amazed that, though they lived around the corner from one another, they were meeting for the first time. Freddie was invited to accompany Smile on the college circuit, where they attracted a modest following playing mostly cover-versions of other group's hits, and the odd original composition.

Later, Smile supported Yes and T Rex, and in February 1969 appeared at the Royal Albert Hall in a charity concert for unmarried mothers: hosted by John Peel, and part of it survives on film. The line-up included such luminaries as Free, Joe Cocker, and the Bonzo Dog Doo Dah Band.

In June 1969 Smile cut their first single at the Trident Studios for the US Mercury label—Tim Staffell's 'Earth', c/w Brian May's 'Step On Me'. Unfortunately, the recording was only issued in America, with hardly any airplay and no support from the record company. It flopped, and the group's other songs for Mercury fell by the wayside because the company had no base in Britain and therefore no contractual rights to release them on home ground. 'Blag', 'Polar Bear' and 'April Lady' resurfaced in 1994 on a bootleg CD, *The Unobtainable Royal Chronicle*. In the Spring of 1970, however, Tim Staffell would leave the group, and after an unsuccessful venture with another outfit, Humpy Bong, he gave up his musical career to concentrate on television special effects. A few years later he worked on the models for *Thomas The Tank Engine*.

Freddie's preoccupation, having witnessed the students' enthusiasm for Smile, was to front a band of his own. He was also desperately unhappy with his home life. His father was virulently opposed to him embarking precociously on a showbiz career, and there were so many arguments that Freddie stayed away from the Feltham house for days and even weeks at a time. Sometimes he would crash down at Roger Taylor's flat in Sinclair Road, or spend the night with two other student friends, Chris Smith and Paul Humberstone, who shared a flat in Kensington.

With his natural charm, wit and infectious personality, Freddie was an all-round favourite, though his aspirations towards greatness must have been wearing at times. Chris Smith, who played briefly with Smile and collaborated with Freddie on some of his earliest songs, remembered how the flamboyant youth had once stood up in a packed London pub and yelled, 'I'm not going to be a star. I'm going to be a *legend*! Tim Staffell recalled:

> Freddie was already a star at college. He exuded confidence in everything he did and was committed to becoming famous. Some people poked fun at him, but he always floored them with a witty response. Freddie developed this camp side of his nature, but at no time was it ever suggested that he was gay. He was never overtly sexual.

In spite of his burning ambition, however, like Brian May and Roger Taylor, Freddie was sensible enough to realize that many such pipe-dreams never pay off. For this reason, he heeded his father's advice, and like his musician friends continued with his studies. May and Taylor gained their respective B.Sc.s, and Freddie left Ealing in the summer of 1969 with a Diploma in Graphic Art and Design. For a little while he tried looking for a job, and through a family friend received a handful of commissions—one was to draw a series of advertisements for lingerie and corsets. The lure of the stage, however, was overpowering, and ignoring his father's pleas he began searching for something that *he* wanted to do.

Thinking that his classical training might give his college chums the impression he was too snooty, he purchased a second-hand guitar and a set of textbooks, then went about learning the basic chords and began working on his first composition—not an easy task, for in those formative years someone had to be close at hand to write down the notes. 'I was learning a lot of things about song structure,' he later recalled. 'As for lyrics, I found *them* quite a task. My strongest point was melody content. I concentrated on this, and the lyrics came afterwards.'

Freddie became actively involved with Ibex, a Liverpudlian group newly arrived in London, who were hoping to make their mark on the college circuit. Ibex comprised Mike Bersin on guitar, Mick 'Miffer' Smith on drums and John 'Tupp' Taylor on bass. All were in their late teens, and they first met Freddie in his and Smile's local pub, in Kensington.

Because none of the trio considered himself a competent vocalist, they reluctantly decided to audition Freddie, whose cod-opera-vocalese improvisations during some of Smile's gigs had not gone unnoticed after he had heckled them for being 'bland and undemonstrative'. He was hired on the spot, mindless of the fact that the other members of the group found his camp demeanour slightly offputting. This campness, of course, he would turn into an art form and become an integral component of his stage persona, without which his future projects would not have been quite so eclectic.

While getting to grips with Ibex, Freddie supplemented his income by setting up a business venture with Roger Taylor selling bric-a-brac, paintings, "quality" second-hand clothes, fur coats and the like in Kensington Market's 'Death Row'—thus named because of its wealth of antique stalls. Freddie was in his element, and in his outlandish garb complimented my multicoloured silk scarves, wide-brimmed hats, feather boas and black-lacquered fingernails fitted in well with the in-crowd. He and Taylor did not make a lot of money, just enough to see them through from one week to the next and to pay for Freddie's 'little foibles', such as his insistence on travelling virtually everywhere by taxi. 'He always looked and acted like a star, though he was penniless,' Brian May recalled, 'He would bring home great bags of stuff, pull out a strip of something and say, "Look at this beautiful garment, it's going to fetch a fortune!" And I'd say, "Fred, it's a piece of *rag*!"'

With Ibex, and *never* in style—the mode of transport being an old Transit van, borrowed from a friend—Freddie travelled up and down England, working in clubs and pubs. In the north there was frequent prejudice on account of the area's homophobia, more often than not incurred by the group's strange appearance. Spray-on satin trousers, velvet and lace shirts, gold-lamé capes and a wealth of plumes were too much for staid, macho environments such as Rochdale and Oldham, though in common with many camp entertainers—Liberace, Danny La Rue, Johnnie Ray—Freddie was a great favourite with 'Bingo Lils' and middle-aged matrons, who only wanted to mother him. 'Roger (Taylor) and I go poncing and ultrablagging just about everywhere,' Freddie wrote to a close friend, Celine Daley, at the end of October from the flat he was now sharing with Smile, in Barnes. 'Lately we're being termed as a couple of queens. Which reminds me that Miffer, the sod, went and told everybody down here that I had seriously turned into a fully-fledged queer.' And if Freddie's friends from these years, in trying to protect his name, have insisted sometimes quite fervently that they saw no evidence of his having homosexual tendencies, Miffer Smith's comments were supported many years later by an admission from Mike Bersin to Andy Davis of *Record Collector*, 'He was kind of straight then. But if he hadn't yet come out of the closet, he was certainly looking through the keyhole.'

Freddie's first professional appearance took place on 23 August 1969, during an afternoon 'bluesology' matinée at Bolton's Octagon Theatre—an event for which no one was paid other than travelling expenses, but to which scores of minor impresarios and working-men's club concert secretaries had been invited. The advertising for these shows stated that any artist or group worthy of their name would be assured of walking off with a clutch of bookings. More often than not, however, the organisers were only after a free show.

Ibex opened their set with 'Lover'—a Freddie and Mike Bersin composition which would reappear, some years later and with its original lines intact, as 'Liar', on Queen's debut album. Performing this, Freddie effortlessly managed to make himself stand out from everyone else on the bill. Ibex's road-manager Ken Testi recalled, 'Everything he did later on stage with Queen, he was doing with Ibex....marching from one end of the stage to the other, from left to right and back again. Stomping about. He brought dynamics, freshness and presentation to the band that had been completely lacking, previously.' And now, without even bothering to ask his name, a photographer from *Bolton Evening News* took several shots of Freddie—his first ever during a public peformance—one of which appeared with the caption, 'One of the performers gets into his stride.'

But even if Freddie appeared to be having fun, he was very much out of his depth in this part of the world. The crunch came after Ibex's visit to Liverpool, where they played the Sink Club, a tiny establishment in the basement of the Rumbling Tum, a seedy greasy-spoon in Hardman Street. Part of their set—a half-hour compilation of Beatles, Jimi Hendrix, Cream and Led Zeppelin songs—was taped by the group's driver, Geoff Higgins, and subsequently appeared on a bootleg CD. Ironically, Smile were also playing in Liverpool that night, at the Green Door, and after their gig they turned up at the Sink Club just in time to join Freddie and his friends on stage—tragically, just as Higgins' tape was running out, robbing the world of what was effectively Queen's début performance, albeit in an unorthodox fashion.

Freddie found Liverpool unpleasant—particularly one evening accosted by a group of drunken skinheads—that he rushed back to London and very nearly threw in the towel. Within days, however, he had bounced back with a brainwave—Ibex had been an unlucky name, so henceforth his outfit would be known as Wreckage. And to prove a point, he personally spray-painted the new name on their instruments and gear.

This move coincided with the departure of the apparently homophobic Mick 'Miffer' Smith. Freddie commented in his letter to Celine Daley, 'Miffer's not with us any more....the bastard just up and left one morning saying he was going to be a milkman back in Widnes.' Smith was replaced with Richard Thompson, the former drummer with 1984.

Wreckage played their first gig at Ealing College on 31 October 1969—the sole evidence of which is one of the fly-posters and a hastily typed setlist which was auctioned by Sotheby's during the summer of 1996. The group supported Iron Butterfly at Imperial College on 5 November, and at several rugby clubs, before staging their farewell concert, just after Christmas at the Wade Dean Grammar School For Girls, where Tupp Taylor's sister was a pupil.

Over the next few weeks, Freddie scoured the music press for audition notices. One, in *Melody Maker*, was for a vocalist with a four-piece blues band, Sour Milk Sea, and took place in Leatherhead, Surrey, on 6 February 1970. Accompanying him for moral support were Roger Taylor and John Harris, Smile's road-manager. Looking like a turn-of-the-century roué in his tightest crimson crushed velvet trousers, boots and fox fur, Freddie breezed into the audition room—a church crypt!—with such panache that he was engaged without anyone showing much interest in what he sounded like.

Sour Milk Sea, so named after the George Harrison song, had been formed in 1968 by ex-public schoolboy Chris Dummett (later Chris Chesney). Very soon Freddie was boasting that he and Dummett were lovers, especially after the pair moved into Smile's flat. 'I had a good relationship with Freddie,' Dummett confessed some years later, while denying that they had had an actual affair. 'We were like Bowie and Ronson, where we related physically to each other on stage.'

On 20 March, Sour Milk Sea played their only important date, a charity gig for Shelter, at Headington's Highfield Parish Hall, when Dummett told Anthony Wood of the *Oxford Mail*, 'I don't feel we are like any other group. Our approach is based on our relationships with one another.' Once again it was Freddie who stole the limelight, as the only one of the group directly facing the camera for their 'publicity shot', which appeared alongside Wood's feature. Needless to say, such favouritism and innocuous narcisism caused friction—and fisticuffs—among the members of Sour Milk Sea. After a handful of further engagements, the outfit folded. So too ended Freddie's friendship with Chris Dummett....a series of events which happened to coincide with Smile's demise.

The trio of May, Taylor and Bulsara were living under the same roof, sharing the same financial hardships and nurturing exactly the same ideas—it was inevitable, therefore, that their best and perhaps only option for success depended upon each other and the combining of their respective, obvious talents. This done, in April 1970 they set about choosing a marketable name for their outfit. May and Taylor drew up a shortlist of two names: Grand Dance, and Rich Kids. Freddie favoured neither, declaring the second choice pretentious, and insisted upon Queen—a name which, with its double connotation of camp and grandeur in this new era of glam-rock, could hardly have been more appropriate.

'We prefer to think of Queen in the regal sense rather than in the queer one,' was how Freddie was still defending his choice, three years later to a stuffy American journalist. 'We never copied *anyone*. Our way was putting together a different kind of theatrical music. Bowie was already doing glam-rock. We *want* to be dandy, we *want* to be shocking and outrageous so that people will *know* whether they like us or not the moment they see us!' May and Taylor offered a weak, futile argument. Such a name was too strong. It might even make them a laughing-stock! Freddie was adamant, however, relying on a mixture of intuition, and the precognitive dream—the fact that all *will* turn out well in the end, so long as this is what one wishes.

Queen it was!

For Queen, the next six months represented a frequently arduous trail of trial and error—auditioning no less than six successive bass-players, not one of whom matched up to the verve and dazzling personality of the group's key figure. The first was Mike Grose, Roger Taylor's pal from St Austell. Grose was particularly useful because he owned a van and some PA equipment -- which the other three could not yet afford—and he thought nothing of leaving his own band, Bent Cement, and trekking up to London to attend the rehearsals which Brian May had organized in an empty lecture hall at Imperial College. The songs, written by May and Freddie, were mostly rehashes of the material they had supplied for Smile and Ibex, and it was with these that they proposed their first concert.

Before this happened, Freddie changed his name—something he had been wanting to do for some time, not just for the sake of his career but to shrug off the shackles of his Colonial past and socially restricted upbringing, and prove to any detractors, most especially his parents and the stuffy members of the tightly knit Parsee community, that here was a force to be reckoned with. Mercury, the Roman god of skill and eloquence, was the ruling planet of his birthsign, Virgo, *and* the messenger of the gods. He had chosen a name which would serve him inordinately well.

The metamorphosis really did enable Freddie to obliterate his past. His close friend David Evans, of whom more later, told me:

> Farouk Bulsara was a name he had buried. He never wanted to talk about any period in his life *before* he became Freddie Mercury, and everything about Freddie Mercury was a self-constructed thing. Like Marlene Dietrich he was a strange double personality—like a rose

grafted on to common stock. If you have a strong enough common stock, it will support the wonderful creature you have created. If it's rotten stock, then the whole thing will collapse.

Several weeks before their split, Smile had been booked by Roger Taylor's mother for a gig in aid of the Red Cross at Truro City Hall. This took place on 27 July 1970, and though newspaper advertisements billed them as Smile, the public were effectively seeing Queen-or at least three-quarters of them—for the first time. They opened with Wreckage's 'Stone Cold Crazy', and the largely rural audience did not quite know what to make of what one journalist described as, 'Four very peculiar-looking gentlemen clad in silk and too many jewels, making enough row to wake half the dead in Cornwall.' Their reception was much warmer a few weeks later, however, when they played Imperial College—the audience was made up mostly of their friends and former classmates. Even so, at the end of July they returned to Cornwall for another gig—and while there parted company with Mike Grose, who since his arrival in London had persistently complained of being homesick.

Grose was replaced by another of Roger Taylor's Cornish friends, Barry Mitchell, who played several small venues with them over the next few months—in and around London, and once travelling to Liverpool, which Freddie found more rewarding than the last trip. On 18 September there was a 'day of mourning' when, not unexpectedly, Jimi Hendrix died of a drugs-overdose, ending the career of the man whom many had feted as the greatest guitarist of the decade. As a mark of respect, Freddie and Roger closed their market stall for the day. Also at around this time, tired of 'slumming it' by sharing accommodation with anyone who happened to be in the neighbourhood, the pair rented a larger flat at 100 Holland Road, in Shepherd's Bush. They were delighted to find a grand piano sitting in the lounge when they moved in—the previous tenant had left it there, unable to get it out of the room!

Early in January 1971, having played with them at the London Marquee and Ewell Technical College, in Surrey, Barry Mitchell more or less left the group in the lurch—although still performing to smallish audiences and earning little over expenses, Queen's diary over the next few months was looking decidedly healthy. Then, just as they were probably thinking they would never have an efficient line-up, Brian May and Roger Taylor were at a college disco when a friend introduced them to John Deacon, a nineteen-year-old Leicester-born bass player and student at Chelsea College who had seen Queen at a Kensington gig the previous October—and *not* been impressed! Now, he was invited to an audition at Imperial College, where he joined in with Freddie's and May's 'Son And Daughter', much to everyone's satisfaction. Thus, by the end of February 1971, Queen were ready for action.

'Home? I don't wanna go home.' (Redferns)

Two: A Magnificent Obsession

When college closed for its summer term, Queen headed off on another tour of Cornwall—organized by Roger, whose brother had found them a tiny cottage to rent, just outside Truro. Taking most of the credit for the venture, he cheekily billed them as 'The Legendary Drummer of Cornwall, Roger Taylor, and Queen'—the 'Queen' printed on playbills in letters smaller than those of his own name. The group fared reasonably well—after the usual pubs and clubs, the tour closed with its first open-air gig at the Tregye Country Club, where they were eighth on a bill of nine. Even so, when they returned to London in the September all four of them still had their feet very firmly on the ground. Still waiting for someone to convince them that they would make enough money to turn professional, Brian and John resumed their studies and later took teaching jobs, while Roger did a volte-face—dropping dentistry to enroll on a course for a degree in biology with the North London Polytechnic. This meant that he had to give up working on his market stall, handing over the reins to Freddie, who shared the running of his business with another stall-holder, Alan Mair.

Queen's biggest break so far occurred early in 1972 when, having recorded a number of demos in the De Lane Lea Studios, Wembley—they were given a job setting up and testing the PA equipment, in return for what they readily assumed would be unlimited studio sessions for themselves—they were heard by Norman Sheffield, an executive from Trident Studios, the company who had earlier signed Smile. Sheffield was overwhelmed by the progress Roger and Brian had made in their playing techniques since then, and he was absolutely bowled over by Freddie's vocal brilliance and the overall quality of the band's demo tape, though it still needed a lot of work doing on it.

Agreeing to take them on, Sheffield persuaded Trident to supply Queen with the PA system they so desperately needed, and to allow them the use of his best studio to rehearse and record the songs for their début album. And still the boys refused to let the notion of success go to their heads. In June, John graduated with a first-class honours degree in electronics, and unwilling to commit himself to a full-time career in music immediately signed for a course which would hopefully gain him his M.Sc. A few weeks later, Roger was awarded his biology degree.

Because the group were compelled to work in studio 'down-time'—when it was not being used by somebody else, most frequently at weekends or in the middle of the night—they spent many hours hanging around corridors and reception rooms, time which they put to good use composing and exchanging ideas. One afternoon, Freddie was introduced to a producer, Robin Cable, who had been in the same studio a few weeks earlier when Phil and Ronnie Spector had been working there.

Cable nurtured two obsessions—the Beach Boys and the famous Spector sound of the Sixties which he now combined by proposing that Freddie record the former's 'I Can Hear Music' in the very distinctive musical style of the latter. The song was taped in a single take, but as Freddie was not satisfied with the overall result—he disliked the synthesizer interlude and the lack of percussion—Brian was brought in to play a guitar harmony, and Roger to enhance it with drums, castanets and tambourine. Without the other two, Freddie then recorded his own arrangement of Dusty Springfield's 'Goin' Back'. Cable took the tape away and everyone forgot about it until the following year, when EMI released the songs on a single. By this time Queen were about to release their début album, so Freddie opted for the pseudonym Larry Lurex. 'My own personal piss-take on Gary Glitter,' he pronounced. Because of this it received little airplay, a great deal of criticism from Glitter fans, and was an unmitigated flop. Currently, the original pressing is one of the most elusive—and costly—items in the Queen back-catalogue.

Until then the group had remained unsalaried and virtually on the breadline—frustrating perhaps for Brian May, who had turned down a research post at the Jodrell Bank Observatory. Then, in mid-September, after much discussion and argument, Trident awarded them a somewhat shabby sum of £80 a week which, they were forced to agree, was at least better than nothing. Two months later they signed an arrangement with the company: Queen would record for Trident, who hopefully would secure them the best possible deal with a reputable record company.

To promote their latest acquisition—they already had Bowie and Elton John, and Carly Simon would follow—T rident organized a gig at the Pheasantry, a large club in Chelsea. This took place on 6 November, and the evening was a disaster. The PA equipment did not arrive until an hour before the performance, and several invited dignitaries from the recording world did not arrive at all. Much better was their gig at the Marquee on 20 December, where besides the songs on their imminent album, Queen set a precedent by performing Elvis Presley's 'Jailhouse Rock'. Their success at the Marquee led to them working more gigs than ever before, and for more money, though they were by no means in the same earnings bracket as many of the other bands on the local circuit. Even so, Roger was able to afford to move out of Freddie's flat into a place of his own in Richmond.

Though they would never be less than the best of friends, the move was welcomed by Freddie. Over the past two years he had grown increasingly close to an ex-date of Brian's: Mary Austin was the 19-year-old manageress of the Biba boutique, one of the last bastions of the 'Swinging Sixties', then in Kensington Church Street, not far from Freddie's market stall.

There has always been considerable speculation as the actual nature of the relationship between Freddie Mercury and Mary Austin, much of it the result of his outspoken comments to the press. If the tabloids were looking for a spicy story, he would always be certain not to disappoint them! This is unimportant, of course. Pretty, blonde, intellectual, calm and collected, Mary moved in with Freddie to become—and remain—not just his closest friend and confidante, but his soul-mate. It was she who advised him on the all-important issues of make-up and fashion, on and off the stage. It was she who stood by him through his every joy, sorrow, success and crisis—even death itself. *That* is what was important. Speaking to *OK* magazine in 2000, Mary recalled:

> He was like no one I had ever met before. He was very confident and I have never been confident. We grew together. I liked him, and it went on from there....Freddie didn't have much money then so we did things like other young people. There were no fancy dinners—they came later when he hit the big time. It took me about three years to really fall in love....The more I got to know him, the more I loved him for himself. He had a quality as a person, which I think is rare in life these days. One thing which was always constant was the love. We knew we could trust each other and we were safe with each other.

Queen's album had been completed by the end of November, and approved by Trident, though there was still a little editing and mixing work to be done on the tracks—and removing a few gremlins which had got on to the tape, which meant that it was not heard by any record company until early in the New Year. Following several rejections, it was taken to the MIDEM Festival, in Cannes, by Trident representative Ronnie Beck. Here, reputedly the only outstanding item in a poor catalogue that year, it was accepted by Roy Featherstone of EMI—one of the companies which had rejected it in the first place.

Meanwhile, to prove their worth with the general public, as opposed to an audience of rowdy drinkers who most of the time just happened to be where Queen were playing, this time the group were invited to participate in Radio One's *Sounds of the Seventies* series—unpaid, though the potential from publicity was enormous. They recorded four songs at the Maida Vale Studios on 5 February 1973, and these were broadcast ten days later: Brian May's revamped version of his and Tim Staffell's 'Doin' Alright', his 'Keep Yourself Alive', and Freddie's evocative 'Liar' and 'My Fairy King' (all produced by Bernie Andrews). Immediately after the broadcast the BBC switchboard was inundated with calls from hundreds of listeners wanting to know more about Queen. A few weeks later, the group signed a contract with EMI for Britain and Europe.

What fascinated everyone most of all was Freddie's voice, with its unusually wide range—escalating within a few bars from a deep, throaty rock-grown to tender, vibrant tenor, then on to a high-pitched coloratura, pure and crystaline in the upper reaches. His highest recorded note, when he was almost forty and his vocal powers were at their peak, would be E above Top C....a phenomenon achieved outside opera only by Yma Sumac and Gracie Fields, and of which he once joked, 'I use the Demis Roussos method. You get a pair of pliers under the frock, and you go *crunch*!' Like Barbra Streisand, he could also cram an astonishing number of words into the briefest bar--' 'Stone Cold Crazy' is a prime example—and still retain perfect diction. Like Piaf he could produce a sob, if the ambiance so dictated.

On 9 April Queen returned to the Marquee. The occasion was a showcase aimed at pleasing Jack Holsen, the managing director of Elektra, the company which would be putting out their records in the United States, providing Holsen liked what he heard. His decision could not have been made easier by the large number of empty seats—many of the invited audience had shunned the event, having been forewarned by the music press that this was just another hype from EMI.

Wearing a black-spangled, skin-tight catsuit, and with the fingernails of one silver-chainmailed hand lacquered black, a pencil-slim Freddie was played on to the stage by Brian May's recently composed instrumental overture, 'Procession'—which Queen had decided to use as an opener for their next album, such was their confidence in their abilities. Preening himself in front of the drum-kit, Freddie minced audaciously from one side of the stage to the other, pausing only to pout or thrust his crotch at the amazed audience in a masterpiece of combined exhibitionism and buffoonery which only he was capable of getting away with and still be taken seriously.

A few days later the first reviews of the gig appeared in the music press, a mixed bag of praise and condemnation. The group alternatively were, 'A bunch of raving poofters trying to jump on to the Bowie bandwagon while doing a poor piss-take of Black Sabbath', or, 'Quite simply breathtaking. *The* band of the future!' Whatever these rags said was, however, of little consequence to Jack Holsen—he had already given Queen the thumbs-up.

Queen's début single, Brian's 'Keep Yourself Alive', c/w his 'Son And Daughter', was released by EMI on 6 July 1973. Against company policy the group had chosen the songs, setting what would be for the next three decades a precedent deciding what or what would not end up on record-store shelves. It is now known that the finicky, prejudiced music press by and large disliked it for no apparent reason than it was different, superior to much of the dross in the pop charts it failed to reach, through lack of air play. *Melody Maker* even had the audacity to admonish, 'Do us *all* a favour, fellas. Change your name to the Uncouth and go on stage in jock-straps!' Only the *New Musical Express*, whose representative had not been at the Marquee, gave them the credit they deserved, declaring, 'If these guys look *half* as good as they sound, they could be huge!'

In anticipation of the group's success, and never one to do things by halves, Freddie had designed their logo, after some consideration plumping for a 'family crest' devised from their birth signs. For Roger and John, both Leo, there were the two lions-rampant flanking the large, crown-enclosed Q, capped by a Cancerian crab (Brian), the whole surmounted by a large phoenix, the symbol of hope and renewed youth. Below the lions, and a deliberate pun, were the two small fairies which Freddie said represented his own sign—Virgo.

The début album, entitled simply *Queen*, was released on 13 July. Produced by John Anthony and Ray Thomas Baker, it had a superb cover photograph by Doug Puddifoot, a friend of Roger's who had covered the group's Cornish tour and taken some interesting shots of Smile. Freddie was depicted in his soon-to-be-classic pose, arms outstretched for an encore, holding aloft the microphone stand, silhouetted from behind by two large, powerful spotlights. In Britain, initially at least, the album was not a resounding success—according to most authorities because it should have been released to coincide with the Marquee showcase, not three months afterwards. In America, however, it sold very well, prompting a New York journalist to fly at once to London to interview the group. 'Queen should be giving glam-rockers like Bowie and the Sweet a run for their money. With one added attraction –musicianship!' Jonathan Singer coyly observed in *Circus*.

Throughout the interview, Freddie fidgeted a lot or used his cuff to polish the spangles on his catsuit, and expressed some concern for the group's future:

We still worry that the name Queen will give people the wrong idea. We want to be a good British regal rock band, and we'll stick to that way of thinking. Our music should override the image because we'll concentrate on putting out good product the whole time. We might get a bit of a pop-tag, but it won't last. We're confident people will take to us because, although the camp image has already been established by Bowie and Bolan, we're taking it to another level.

It was a supreme example of inefficient publicity which inadvertently gave Queen their big break. The copy of the album sent to Mike Appleton, the producer of BBC2's legendary *The Old Grey Whistle Test*, had neither label nor publicity handout. Thus, not knowing who or what he was playing, but impressed just the same—he later swore that he had not heard the single—Appleton included it in the programme which went out on 24 July, over a piece of animated footage of Franklin D Roosevelt's wartime presidential election campaign. Needless to say, Appleton received a number of urgent calls—including an irate one from a Trident executive—and the next day Queen found themselves whisked off to Broadcasting House to tape four songs for Radio One's top-rating showcase, *The John Peel Show*. Besides the two songs from the single, they re-recorded 'Liar' from the album, and a new song, 'See What A Fool I've Been'.

A few days later the quartet began working on a short film at Shepperton Studios, commissioned by Trident to promote their album in Europe and the United States—*Queen* was to be released there on 4 September. Freddie, who had been told by director Mike Mansfield to think up a marketable gimmick, as usual went over the top—he shaved his very hirsute chest! Filming was an unpleasant, unnatural experience for them all. They had never mimed before—and grew frustrated during 'Liar' when the tempo rose and it was almost impossible to keep in synch while the cameramen were constantly bumping into them in their attempts to film from as many awkward angles as possible. Also, the sets were white when Freddie had emphasised they should be black—a *truc* often used on the Continent by contemporaries Johnny Halliday and Eddie Mitchell. After a few tantrums from both sides, Mansfield was shown the door and, directed by Queen themselves—setting yet another precedent—the project was completed the way they wanted it. Trident then assigned them their first publicist, Tony Brainsby, who had worked with such diverse acts as Cat Stevens, Paul McCartney and Mott The Hoople.

Queen were now working hard on their second album, *Queen II*, though at their own pace now that Trident had given them their own studio—and issued a press statement to the effect that the group had no option but to make it because they had already set the company back in excess of £60,000. On 13 September their performance at the Golders Green Hippodrome was taped for Radio One's *In Concert* series: the programme went out the following month. Trident then set about planning the group's first national tour of theatres, as opposed to clubs and pubs, a Herculean task which attained fruition only when a great deal of money exchanged hands between the company and Bob Hirschmann, the manager of American rock-band Mott The Hoople, whom they eventually supported. Hirschmann had been unwilling to take on Queen, it emerged, because their first single, 'Keep Yourself Alive', had failed to chart in the United States and the money—at the time claimed to be for financing Queen's PA equipment and spectacular lighting –was in effect a thinly disguised insurance policy, just in case they failed to make the grade.

The try-outs for the tour took Queen to Europe. In Paris they performed on France-Inter's long-running radio show, *Pop-Club*, hosted by José Artur. Then, after several gigs, radio and television programmes in Belgium and Holland, the group played their first open-air concert at the Frankfurt Bagodesburg. While in Germany Freddie paid a clandestine visit to one of the city's notorious leather bars which offered him a taste of the overt gay macho culture which, a few years later, he would triumphantly bring to the stage. Upon the group's return to England, besides a rip-roaring performance at London's Paris Theatre, there were two gigs at Imperial College—the one of 2 November being Queen's first sell-out performance.

The tour kicked off at Leeds Town Hall on 12 November, where Queen performed numbers from their début album, tested the water with tracks from their forthcoming one, and tossed in a few standards such as 'Big Spender', the song from *Sweet Charity* which had been a big hit for Shirley Bassey and Peggy Lee. For this, Freddie was at his most outrageous, strutting about the stage like a peacock and encouraging the audience to join in with the refrain. There were innumerable reviews on the music press, again mostly bad. As would happen with the Morrissey concerts of the Nineties, some of these hack journalists appear to have witnessed an entirely different performance from the one the fans had seen, and like to think that they were intelligently dissecting it, when in reality they were less interested in the music than they were in making personal remarks about the artists. The quartet took it in their stride, adopting the maxim, 'Better to be kicked than ignored completely.' And in any case, as the tour progressed through nineteen further venues, it became increasingly obvious that their fan base was swelling at an incredible but welcome rate—that audiences of *all* ages were more interested in seeing this exciting new band than the one topping the bill, and not at all interested in what the detractors had to say. So many people turned up *just* to see Queen, but also ended up becoming Mott The Hoople fans, that the latter's management insisted that Queen should also support them on their 1974 American tour. Naturally, there were no arguments!

On 3 December 1973, the day after their penultimate concert at Chatham Central, Queen taped their second session for the BBC's *Sounds of the Seventies*, with Bernie Andrews. This time they chose 'Son And Daughter', 'Great King Rat', and 'Modern Times Rock 'N' Roll' from their first album, and 'Ogre Battle' from its soon-to-be-released successor. The eight songs from the sessions remained in the BBC archives for another sixteen years, when they were put out on the album *Queen At The Beeb*. Then, as in 1973, it was Freddie's 'Ogre Battle' which received the most accolades. 'A panorama of virulent grandeur and broadsword clashing mania,' was how Malcolm Dome of *RAW* magazine reviewed it, while Paul Elliot of *Sounds* perceived the whole concept as, 'Quaint, plush, pompous, ritzy-kitsch de-luxe metal....Spartacus in sequins!'

With *Queen II* completed, at the end of January 1974 the group flew to Australia for two concerts at the Sunbury Music Festival, near Melbourne. The brief tour was a disaster. Brian was suffering the after-effects of a gangrenous infection in his arm, brought about by a dirty needle used during the mandatory inoculations for the trip. Freddie had tinnitus and could not hear properly. At Sunbury there was a great deal of bitchiness in the promoter's camp on account of the hype which Queen awarded themselves—driving everywhere in a hired limo, while the other acts had to stick to battered old vans, and turning up for photo-shoots looking immaculate but very much out of place in silks and velvets when everyone else was wearing T-shirts and jeans. Freddie told one surprised journalist, 'We're not trying to be different. If you're a professional, darling, you don't have to *try* to do anything!'

The worst came when Queen were introduced on stage by a famous chat-show host who—not content with leading the crowd into a slow-handclap—bared his buttocks, loudly broke wind into the microphone and pronounced, 'That's what *I* think of those stuck-up Pommie bastards!' Those closest to the stage did actually enjoy Queen's set, brief as this was: halfway through, the lighting-rig exploded, plunging the stage into total darkness. It had been sabotaged by local electricians, angry with the group for having brought out their own crew instead of using the on-site workforce. Not surprisingly, Queen cancelled the next evening's show—the 'official' reason being that Brian and Freddie were indisposed—and a few days later, at their own expense, they and their entourage flew home to England. At Heathrow their plane was met by a bevvy of reporters and press photographers who had been misinformed that it was *the* Queen who was arriving! Freddie posed and pouted, but he and the rest of the group were ignored, barring one reporter who dismissed them as 'a bunch of long-haired layabouts'.

In February, in a decision which must have shocked the music press, the readers of *New Musical Express* voted Queen runners-up (after Leo Sayer) for 'Most Promising New Name'—odd considering they had had had no chart success whatsoever, though this was remedied at the end of the month when EMI distributed promotional copies of 'Seven Seas Of Rhye' c/w 'See What A Fool I've Been'. The song had appeared on their first album, but this longer, updated version was to be on *Queen II*.

The group were taken under the wing of Ronnie Fowler, the head of EMI's promotions department—who just happened to be one of their biggest fans. For several days, Fowler pestered radio and television producers, and his coup paid off when on 21 February—as a result of the promotional film for David Bowie's 'Rebel, Rebel' failing to get to the studio on time—Queen were offered a last-minute spot on *Top of the Pops*. Therefore—in the days when the pop-show actually made the ratings—millions of viewers were treated to what the *Sunday Times* called, 'Led Zeppelin in frocks' contribution to glam-rock....pure Freddie Mercury, massively entertaining, superbly artificial and enigmatic to the point of meaninglessness!'

Television audiences certainly had seen nothing quite like this since the days of the outrageous New York Dolls. With his almost androgynous porcelain features framed by a curtain of dark, silky hair, and sporting an excruciatingly tight catsuit which revealed a generous expanse of hirsute torso, this particular frontman was ten times more exciting—not to mention talented—than any other of the past two decades.

Henceforth, for Queen it would be roses all the way. Such was the demand for the single that EMI were given just two days to get it into the shops. Radio One played it to death, and within a matter of weeks it had peaked at Number 10 in the charts—and Queen were planning their first headlining tour. As for the 'Led Zeppelin connection', John Deacon, the least vociferous member of the group, angrily kicked this into touch by telling the press, '*We're* more structured, and a lot more intricate planning goes into *our* music, especially in the recording studio!"

Queen's success resulted in Freddie giving up his stall on Kensington Market, not that he had spent much time working there of late. Rehearsals for the tour took place at Ealing Studios, with all the stops pulled out to ensure its success in a climate which was financially unsound—Britain had been hit by the three-day week and the oil crisis. *Queen II* had been scheduled for release ahead of the 22-date tour—this began on 1 March at Blackpool's Winter Garden Theatre—but because of a government restriction on electricity it did not come out until eight days later. *Record Mirror* called it 'the dregs of glam-rock' and concluded, 'If *this* band are our *brightest* hope for the future, we're committing rock and roll suicide.' Other music press publications were similarly dismissive.

The fans, of course, proved the press wrong each evening by chanting 'God Save The Queen' before the group went on stage, and by screaming for encores after they had left. Trident and EMI received hundreds of letters of support, leading to the creation of an official fan club, set up and run initially by Pat and Sue Johnstone, two of Roger's friends from Truro. The fans also rushed out to buy the new album, which soared to Number 5 in the charts, while the re-released *Queen* peaked at Number 24. Both albums remained in the charts for over six months.

The tour had its share of incidents, some caused by fans, others aggravated by the group themselves. At Stirling University on 16 March, a brawl erupted in the auditorium after the concert, when an exhausted Queen did not make it into their fourth encore, and two fans were stabbed though not seriously injured. Ten days later, at a post-gig party in their hotel on the Isle of Man, drunken revelers smashed up the room and Queen were told by the island authorities, 'We never want to see you or your people here again.'

The tour should have ended on 31 March with a gig at the Rainbow Theatre, in London's Finsbury Park. However, because of the fracas in Stirling, the 17 March show at Barbarella's nightclub in Birmingham had been postponed—ostensibly to allow the rough element among the group's camp-followers to settle down—and it now took place on 2 April. Here, following a 'dare' from Roger Taylor, two members of Queen's road crew and the lead singer from the support band, Nutz, added mayem to the proceedings by streaking several times across the stage.

Queen's first American tour, supporting Mott The Hoople, opened in Denver on 16 April where the local red-necks, unaccustomed to seeing their rock stars in Zandra Rhodes silks, nail varnish and make-up, initially regarded them as a joke. Gradually, however, they gained momentum and press approval until 7 May, when they began a six-night stint on Broadway. The venue was the plush Uris Theater, famous for its Tennessee Williams and Rachel Crothers social dramas, but thus far in its history never host to a rock concert. All should have been well. The entire week was a sell-out, Queen were sensational, and the reviews mostly good. Unlike their British counterparts the American press never mounted a smear campaign against the group. However, the fans made a nuisance of themselves, causing thousands of dollars' worth of damage by urinating in the auditorium, and completely ruining the beautiful old carpets by putting their cigarettes out on them. As with the Isle of Man, Queen were told never to darken the sidewalks of Broadway again.

Queen might have been able to cope with this drama –they did after all pay for all the damage caused by someone else—had it not been for the sudden curtailment of the tour. Just as they were doing well, Brian May collapsed with what was initially thought to be food poisoning. It was much worse than this: hepatitis, allegedly as a result of the same infected needle which had caused all the trouble on the eve of the Australian trip.

The group returned to England in the middle of May, having promised to resume the American tour later in the year. Brian was hospitalized for four weeks, initially in a critical condition. There then followed a mad dash to inoculate everyone who had been in contact with him during the last few months. Even so, Brian steadfastly refused to vegetate, and from his sickbed worked on the new songs for Queen's next album, *Sheer Heart Attack*.

Once Brian was back on his feet, the group began working in the studio. Then in August, when the album was almost complete, he was taken ill again—this time with a perforated ulcer, and rushed to King's College Hospital, where surgeons carried out an emergency operation. He came out of the hospital with enough time to spare to overdub those small sections of the album where, due to illness, his playing had been below par, before attending a reception on 5 September at London's Café Royal. This was Freddie's 28th birthday, and the group was presented with a silver disc for selling 100,000 copies of *Queen II*. They received the accolade from Queen Elizabeth II lookalike Jeanette Charles, and Freddie quipped, 'You'd think she'd have gone all the way and invited us to Buckingham Palace!'

On 11 October, two tracks from *Sheer Heart Attack* were released on a double-A side: 'Killer Queen' and 'Flick Of The Wrist', both written by Freddie. The single recompensed all their hard work by peaking at Number 2 in the British charts, and gave Queen their first Top Twenty hit in the United States. It was also a hit in several European countries. In France, 'Killer Queen' became that winter's gay anthem. At the Piano-Zinc in Paris—an establishment where entry was free so long as one got up and 'did a turn'—dozens of Freddie lookalikes performed it *a capella*, stopping the show every night for weeks. The journalist Alain Lavanne, confessing that this was his favourite Queen song, called it, 'A copulation of hard-on guitars and vagina vocals which gives off a heady, forbidden perfume before exploding into a steamhammering orgasm!'

As there was now no question of them returning to the United States before early 1975, Queen embarked on an 18-date British tour which opened at Manchester's Palace Theatre on 30 October. Each meticulously rehearsed show began 'Continental-style'—the stage area plunged into total darkness, a brief overture, and Freddie's materialization in a single spotlight to deliver the first few bars of 'Now I'm Here' before the rest of the group joined in.

Then on their set rapidly gained momentum—fireworks, dry ice and spectacular effects from the huge new lighting-rig. Julianne Regan, the singer with the disbanded group, All About Eve, saw Queen for the first time on 3 November at Coventry's Apollo Theatre. 'I thought he was gorgeous,' she said of Freddie,

"I loved the way he flicked his wrists when he played the piano. He was a jamboree bag of After Eight Mints, champagne, red rose, satin and silver—tastefully tacky and immensely talented, an absolute bundle of charisma and the unsurpassable king of weird and wonderful vocal harmonies.'

The fans were generally better behaved during this tour than the previous one, though there were problems in Glasgow on 8 November. This was the day *Sheer Heart Attack* was released, and several overzealous fans grabbed Freddie when he moved too close to the edge of the stage, pulling him head first into the pit. Luckily he was unhurt, though after the show ten rows of seats were completely destroyed. However, rather than present Queen with a bill for damages, the manager of the Apollo handed each member of the group a silver statuette—for the first time ever, HOUSE FULL notices had graced its hoardings.

The tour should have ended on 19 November with Queen's gig at the Rainbow—their only London concert—but such was the demand for tickets that the promoters tagged on an extra performance for the following evening. Both shows were filmed: the 30-minute *Queen At The Rainbow* was shown in provincial cinemas in 1976, supporting the Burt Reynolds film *Hustle*, while the complete version was only ever included in the mail-order only *Box Of Tricks*, issued in 1992, and way beyond the price-range of most fans. The tape-recording, intended for use on a live album, was archived by Trident, who believed that fans who had bought Queen's three albums would complain of being ripped off by buying the same songs again.

Many people believed that Trident were the ones doing the ripping off. Though they travelled, lodged, ate and even had fun in great style, Queen were still only getting £80 each per week from their management, who had recently bought *their* second Rolls-Royce! 'Theirs was an impossible situation,' said Barbara Baker, their producer's wife. 'Freddie wanted to buy a piano, and

John Deacon needed just £2,000 for the deposit on a little house because he was getting married. And Norman Sheffield would say, "Who do you think you *are? We can't give you the *money!*"' For the time being, however, an uneasy truce was maintained.

Three days after the Rainbow, Queen flew to Sweden for a concert in Gothenberg, followed by dates in Finland, Belgium, Germany, Holland and Spain. There were ten shows—others were cancelled when the PA truck was involved in an accident—but each one was a sell-out, the 6,500 tickets for Barcelona being snapped up in mere hours, causing Freddie to fall in love in the city which, some years later, would become synonymous with his name.

Queen returned to the United States at the end of January 1975, two weeks after John Deacon's marriage to his long-time girlfriend, Veronica Tetzlaff. Their second single from the album, 'Now I'm Here', c/w 'Lily Of The Valley', had entered the British charts, where it reached Number 11. This time there was no doubting their success—all thirty shows sold out in advance, and additional dates were tagged on as the tour progressed, sometimes involving two performances in the same day. Early in April, Queen crossed the border for two concerts in Canada.

For Freddie, who had developed a throat infection ten days into the tour—a problem which would bug him for the rest of his life, on account of too much on-stage shouting and too many cigarettes—the experience was a triumph of mind over matter. There were times when his doctors forbade him to speak, let alone sing, advice he invariably ignored, and Queen were fortunate in that only a few dates had to be cancelled. The tour ended in Seattle on 6 April, after which the group flew to Hawaii—their first holiday together—to wind down in preparation for their first visit to Japan.

Freddie, who even this early in his career had developed an aversion for speaking about his private life—wishing to avoid the sneers of the British music press—had come very close to being 'outed' while in Ohio, early in February. The American press (and for the time being their British counterparts) knew absolutely nothing about his discreet post-gig forays into the gay scene of each town or city on the tour circuit and that, unable to do so in Ohio, he had 'bought in' from an agency specialising in such things. Thus when he was interviewed by David Hancock of the fortunately obscure *Record Popswop Mirror*, he almost came unstuck when Hancock was shown into his hotel room thirty minutes early—to find Freddie reclining on a pile of cushions, being waited on hand and foot by a trio of scantily clad muscular hunks. The reporter—in his feature he referred to Freddie as 'The Quicksilver Girl'—was curious to know why he was apparently incapable of fixing himself a drink or even of lighting his own cigarettes. Nothing was mentioned about the real reason for the young men being there. Freddie told Hancock, expecting to be believed,

> They're servants, dear. I just love being pampered. It's just something that's grown with me. I can't even make myself a cup of tea. I'm useless at it, so I have someone else to do it for me. That's the kind of environment I live in, my dear!

46

'D'amor sull'ali rosee.' (Bret/Cinemago, Paris)

Three: Hero Of The Ginza

When Queen arrived in Tokyo on 18 April 1975, both *Sheer Heart Attack* and 'Killer Queen' were in the lower reaches of the Japanese charts, and at the airport they were mobbed 3,000 screaming fans—something which was yet to happen in Britain and the United States. 'Suddenly, we were the Beatles,' Brian reflected. 'We literally had to be carried over the heads of these kids....this wasn't a rock band thing, this was being a teen idol.'

The idolatry, in fact, had less to do with them being Queen than with the Japanese's love of great camp icons. The *tragédiennes* of French song—with the exception of Edith Piaf, who refused to perform there because of the country's wartime atrocities—have all been immensely successful there. In 1975, twenty-five years after her last tour of Japan, the réaliste singer Damia (1889-1978), who Freddie greatly admired, was still getting into the charts with her songs of tormented love, suicide and despair. And Freddie, with his over-the-top dramatics—one Japanese newspaper described him as 'a cross between *kabuki* and *le cinéma muet'*—was like Bowie, Elton John, Marc Almond and the later Morrissey in every sense a drama-queen, something he admitted himself.

The first of Queen's eight concerts in Japan took place the following evening at the immense, 10,000-seater Budokan, a stadium usually reserved for martial arts, where the management had dispensed with the usual type of security and had employed thirty Sumo wrestlers to prevent fans from getting too close to the stage. They proved useless against the ensuing pandemonium where several hundred mostly teenage girls surged forward in a massive wave, flattening the flimsy seating and scrambling over the wrestlers. The instant Freddie raised his hand, as if warding off a blow, they all retreated to what was left of their seats.

The tour progressed with equal hysteria through Nagoya, Kobe, Fukuoka—'And the same to you, dear!', was Freddie's response the first time he heard the name—Okayama, Shizuoka and Yokohama. Each member of the group had his own personal bodyguard, and for their own safety they travelled between venues in armoured cars or vans. Everywhere they went they were showered with gifts—mostly flowers, but occasionally expensive items, such as the lovely kimonos they wore for their return to the Budokan on 1 May for their farewell concert—by which time both their album and single were topping the Japanese charts.

Freddie developed two passions while in Japan: art and geisha boys. Jacky Gunn, who co-runs the Queen Fan Club, told me:

> Anything Japanese, Fred would buy it. It started off with small things he could bring through customs without paying the duty. As he became richer, he bought more. Statuettes, paintings, screens, dolls. You name it, he bought it. One year he bought us all the most beautiful silk kimonos. He was always generous, always kind to his friends.

Freddie's second fascination was for the world of the Ginza, the lively and colourful thoroughfare in Tokyo long favoured by both tourists and artists, almost a Japanese Pigalle or Soho. During this and every subsequent stay in the city, he made discreet visits to the notorious but classy *kagé-me-jaya* (tea-houses in the shadows), founded after World War II by American GIs, where for the appropriate fee customers were able to sample the delights of one or more of the geisha boys whose names appeared on the menu, next to the food. He met Japan's most celebrated female impersonator, 42-year-old Miwa (Akihuro Maruyama). Exquisitely beautiful and known as 'The Japanese Piaf', Miwa ran his own cabaret in the Ginza, and in the late-Seventies started adding Freddie Mercury songs to his very extensive repertoire, as a tribute to Freddie's importance to the *kagé-me-jaya* community.

Miwa always maintained that, more than any other entertainer, Freddie epitomised the archetypal *gai-jin*, as foreigners are called in Japan, because Western men are usually bigger, better-endowed and more hirsute than their Oriental counterparts. But if any of these geisha boys were hoping to add Freddie's name to their list of clientele, they would be sorely disappointed. According to his friends, he would have absolutely no amorous interest in what he called 'the little people': he simply liked them to pamper him and wait on him hand and foot.

Returning to England, Queen coped with the growing burden of their management and financial problems by immediately getting to work on their next album. All four members of the group were deeply in debt to sound and lighting companies. John Deacon in particular was finding it hard making ends meet, still living in a bedsit, and with a baby on the way—his son, Robert, was born in July. Yet their popularity in Britain had only escalated during their overseas trip. The readers of *Disc* had voted them Best British, International & Live Group, and 'Killer Queen' best single. On 22 May Freddie received an Ivor Novello Award for the song, causing a rumpus among the other nominees, who did not believe that pop-songs warranted such accolades. In Belgium the song won a prestigious *Lion d'or*, yet Trident's seemingly feeble excuse for not awarding the group a pay-rise was that sending them around the world had cost the company too much money already—£200,000, they claimed. They were therefore left with no alternative than to place the matter in the hands of their lawyer, Jim Beach.

Freddie's lover at this time was David Minns, a dark-haired, well-built man who had worked for Paul and Linda McCartney for a while before turning toward music publishing. Minns had of

50

late taken a young singer-songwriter under his wing: Eddie Howell had already released three singles and a promising début album, *The Eddie Howell Gramophone Record*. Now, in between composing material for Queen's new album, Freddie began showing an avid interest in Howell's career. Having listened to the demo of 'The Man From Manhattan', a song about the Mafia, Freddie announced that he would like to produce it.

Howell was invited to the Holland Road flat, where after going through the song once on his grand piano Freddie decided that he also wanted to sing the backing vocals. Not only this, he persuaded Brian May to provide lead guitar and Mike Stone—Queen's recording engineer—was roped into the project as well. The recording sessions took place at the Sarm Studios, but dragged on for almost a week on account of Freddie's meticulous attention to detail—in one instance, a single note D which ended the song, when any number of substitutes would have sufficed. Not to be thwarted, Freddie spent £800 of his own money on a motorcycle courier who scoured London's music shops until a suitable bell could be found for a certain point of the orchestration. He then told his friend, 'If this isn't a hit, dear, you should sue Warner Brothers!' Though successful in parts of Europe, the record proved a costly flop in Britain—not because it was mediocre, but because Eddie Howell's bass player was not British and a member of the UK Musicians Union, which saw the record banned from the airwaves.

At the end of August, Queen were able to break free of their contract with Trident—though at a staggering cost. In order to record directly for EMI, they were compelled to sign a severance contract with Trident, the terms of which were an immediate down-payment of £100,000—which they did not even have a fraction of—and one per cent of the royalties from their next six albums. Freddie told *New Musical Express*, 'As far as Queen are concerned, our old management is deceased. They cease to exist in any capacity with us whatsoever. One leaves them behind like one leaves excreta. We feel so relieved!' Trident reciprocated by dumping the group's PA equipment in an alley outside the studio—in the rain.

Queen also dispensed with the services of their publicist, Tony Brainsby, and aided by Jim Beach—now a close friend—began a frantic search for a new manager. After several setbacks they settled for John Reid, then managing Elton John. He offered sound advice: the group should leave their financial problems to the experts—his lawyers—and get on with what they were good at: making records. Reid and John Beach entered into negotiations with EMI and quickly persuaded them to advance Queen the money to pay off their 'debt' to Trident, though their troubles with this company would continue for a little longer. The deal was clinched with a lavish party on 19 September at the London Coliseum, where the group was presented with a selection of gold and silver discs for all three of their albums, as well as for 'Killer Queen'.

Queen's new album was given the title *A Night At The Opera*, after the classic Marx Brothers' comedy film, and its pre-publicity proclaimed it one of the most expensive albums ever made—at an estimated cost of £35,000. It took three months to record, in six different studios, and with a great deal of the in-production tension and tantrums which perfectionism invariably creates. Unquestionably, its *piece de résistance* was Freddie's 'Bohemian Rhapsody', a pioneering rock *symphonie en miniature*, almost six minutes long, which took three weeks to record, and which he insisted would be Queen's next single. Their management was wholly against the idea. It was twice the length of an average single, they declared, and would never get any air-play. Freddie recalled in *Rockline* some years later, 'They wanted to chop it down to three minutes. I said, "It either stays as it is, or forget it!" It was either going to be a big flop or a big hit.

A risk element is always involved and that's the way I like it. That's what makes good music.'

The single was released on 31 October, backed with Roger Taylor's 'I'm In Love With My Car' and attractively packaged in Queen's first ever British picture sleeve—and the rest is, to borrow an old cliché, history. On 7 November, seven days before the group's new British tour, it and the album were premiered for the largely indifferent media at London's Roundhouse Studios. Freddie's pal Kenny Everett played it fourteen times during two consecutive weekend shows on Capital Radio, and it shot straight up the charts, holding the Number One slot for nine weeks—beating the record set in 1957 by Paul Anka's 'Diana'. Everett recalled the first time he heard it:

> Freddie plonked it on the machine, and this glorious operatic wonder came out. I remember him being unsure about this pile of genius—it was like Mozart saying he didn't know if his clarinet concerto was going to take off. 'Bohemian Rhapsody' had Number One written all over it from the first note.

The song won Queen their first platinum disc, a British Phonographic Industry Award for Best Single of 1975, a second Ivor Novello Award for Freddie and, if this were not enough, at the 1977 Brit Awards is was named joint Best Pop Single of the Last Twenty-Five years with Procul Harum's 'A Whiter Shade Of Pale'.

'Bohemian Rhapsody' also set another invaluable precedent, a trend without which today's pop industry would be virtually useless—the promotional video. Promotional films, of course, were nothing new in the music business. Badly edited fragments of monochrome film survive from the American jazz age, badly out of synch, and French music-hall star Marie Dubas had used a a film-clip in 1936 to promote her million-selling 'Mon légionnaire', a song which Freddie adored in the cover version by Edith Piaf. Today, the videos are sadly more often than not much more interesting than the songs they promote—Adam & The Ants 'Prince Charming', for example, with its brilliant cameo featuring Diana Dors, means nothing unless seen. But Queen's video for 'Bohemian Rhapsody' was the very first time a pop song had used the medium.

Freddie's contribution to this masterpiece was pure Grand Guignol—hunching his slender frame over the grand piano in a parody of Paderewski, crossing his hands while raising them from the keys to an absurd level with his chin. The original plan was that the video should be used as a stand-in should Queen be too busy touring to appear on *Top of the Pops*. It was directed by Bruce Gower, the man responsible for *Queen At The Rainbow*, and was filmed at Elstree in four hours, for just £4,500, a mere drop in the ocean compared with some less presentable modern day 'epics', but it was a major contributory factor towards the song's staggering success around the world. 'Try making *that* on your Super-8 at home!' enthused the DJ Dave Lee Travis, after it had received its television premiere, and in its entirety. The video also offered Queen something they had never had before—a silhouette, in this instance a conjoined, quadruple head-and-shoulders shot of them gazing up into a spotlight, which became almost as synonymous to their image as Freddie's crest.

The great mystery surrounding 'Bo Rap', as it affectionately known by fans, is that no one really knew what it was about. Moreover, its composer was reticent when speaking about it, saying, 'I want people to listen to it, think about it, and then decide for themselves what it means to them.' The music-press, of course, could not leave it there and, fourteen years after its release would still be pulling it to pieces.

The *New Musical Express*, borrowing a line from the song, devised a regular feature entitled 'BISMILLAH...NO! We Will Not Let Him Go: The World's Worst Lyrics', in which musically challenged 'experts'—denounced by as 'wankers' by Freddie—panned such standards as Bobby Goldsboro's 'Honey', Band Aid's 'Feed The World', and even Elvis Presley's 'Jailhouse Rock'.

The opening song on *A Night At The Opera*, 'Death On Two Legs', caused Queen untold problems when Trident executive Norman Sheffield saw the bracketed subtitle, 'Dedicated to...', and listened to lines such as 'You suck my blood like a leech/ You've taken all my money and you want more!', he knew only too well that the words were directed at him. Worse still were the 'sewer rat' and 'barrow-boy' references and the damning, 'But now you can kiss my ass goodbye!' Needless to say, there was soon talk of an injunction preventing the album's release—or at least the removal of this song.

The group stood their ground. Though the lyrics were autobiographical, no lawyer would have been able to prove that they were an attack against Trident, though EMI are alleged to have paid the company a large sum of hush money to persuade them to drop their action, which they did. Gary Langan, a record producer who worked with Queen on *Sheer Heart Attack* and their next three albums, remembered the actual recording session and recalled how Freddie had worked himself up into such a fury that 'blood had come out of his ears'. He added, 'No one would ever believe how much hate and venom went into both the singing of that song, let alone the lyrics themselves.'

Queen's now annual tour opened at the Liverpool Empire on 14 November 1975. The costumes were more outrageous than ever before and different for almost every show, the lighting more spectacular and costly, the music louder and more evocative. Some nights, Freddie wore one of the kimonos he had

55

brought back from Japan, or just multicoloured tights which left absolutely nothing to the imagination—and left many people wondering if he really *was* gay, or just having everyone on. It was at around this time, too, that he began doing exciting things with his detachable microphone stand, turning it into an essential prop. It would ably serve as barbell, guitar, golf-club, hatchet, baton, neck-exerciser—and penis extension!

Acknowledging that Queen were now the biggest band in Britain, James Johnson of the *London Evening Standard* interviewed Freddie in Birmingham on 10 December and asked him, quite bluntly, if his 'camp demeanour' was really a part of his personality. The singer's response was equally to the point, and not a 'dear' in sight. He also threw in another thinly veiled reference to Queen's tribulations with Trident for good measure:

> Are you asking whether I'm bisexual? If I told you, it would destroy all the mystery. I move in a theatrical world and people can draw their own connotations from that. I have a girlfriend I have lived with for five years....You have to be prepared to build up a defense if you're really into it for the big time, otherwise you get eaten up. I always say that success has changed me because it's made me vicious....the whole group have become more vicious, more calculating.

Freddie's almost ruthless perfectionism was a constant theme running throughout David Evans' 1992 biography, *This Is The Real Life*, co-written with David Minns and drawing on innumerable reminiscences from friends, fans and colleagues. Evans, who had worked for John Reid Enterprises in the capacity of general manager, observed, 'He was the sort of man you're thrilled to have as a friend, but desperately relieved not to wake up next to on a bad morning.'

The Metropolis Studios' Gary Langan, who worked with Queen on four of their albums. recalled in the same publication that, on account of his mood-swings, Freddie could be quite frightening as a person: 'He wasn't very approachable. If you were going to be his friend, you knew it was going to be something you had to work on....A friendship with Freddie was not something that he was going to accept at a glance.'

Meanwhile, each venue on the 1975 tour-circuit was a complete sell-out, and there was little trouble with fans. There was one incident after their show in Newcastle on 11 December when, according to the local police, 'an interested party' tipped them off that the group were carrying drugs. Their coach was stopped outside Dundee, where they were escorted to the nearest station and searched. The police must have been truly disappointed to find only a small bottle of headache pills.

The tour should have ended on 23 December, but at the end of November Queen had played a four-night stint at London's Hammersmith Odeon which had proved so successful that on Christmas Eve they returned here for a concert which was broadcast live on both Radio One and BBC2's *The Old Grey Whistle Test*. The event was doubly important for Freddie and Brian May, whose parents were in the audience. Like their sons, they had been virtual neighbours for years and were now meeting for the first time. Exactly what Bomi and Jer Bulsara thought of their son, camping it up to the nines in front of thousands of ecstatic fans is anybody's guess—not to mention all the mincing, effing and blinding which occurred during the post-gig party. They did, however, put on a tremendous show of good manners and correct etiquette which impressed everyone, and shared in their son's delight when *A Night At The Opera*, released on 21 November, reached Number One not long afterwards.

Queen's long-overdue American tour began on 27 January 1976 at the Palace Theater in Waterbury, Connecticut, where the

57

audiences were confused by their opening number, 'Now I'm Here'. The lines were alternated by Freddie and the group's personal assistant Pete Brown miming to his voice, the pair standing at opposite ends of the stage and wearing identical costumes. As with their previous visit to the United States, it took over a week for the tour to gather momentum. Freddie refused to socialize with company executives and record promoters, attending only the post-gig parties he had personally organized, and neither 'Bohemian Rhapsody' nor *A Night At The Opera* were getting sufficient air-play, though by 5 February this had been rectified when Queen played the first of four gigs at New York's Beacon Theater. The single reached Number 9 in the charts and the album Number 4. Also while in New York they bumped into Ian Hunter of Mott The Hoople, who persuaded them to harmonize on 'You Nearly Done Me In', one of the tracks from his forthcoming solo album. And towards the end of the 33-date tour, the group received the welcoming news that all four of their albums were currently in the British charts.

After America, Queen flew to Japan for eleven concerts. They had learned several phrases phonetically in Japanese, and very nearly caused a riot at the Budokan the first time Freddie pronounced one of them. From Japan they flew to Australia, for a part of their contract which they had been reluctant to fulfil. This time, however, there was only enthusiasm. The vulgar television presenter was nowhere to be seen, each of their eight shows had been sold out for weeks, and both their album and single were topping the charts. At the end of April they returned to England to begin working on their next album, and on 29 May Brian married his sweetheart, Chrissy Mullen, at the Roman Catholic Church in Barnes.

At around this time, British newspapers began speculating over cracks which they claimed had begun appearing in Freddie's relationship with Mary Austin–according to the tabloids, because he had recently confessed his bisexuality to her. This, and further press allegations that Mary was beginning to find him an embarrassment, could only of course have been pure fabrication. During the summer of 1976 Freddie's antics were no more over-the-top than they had been years before when Mary had first met him—and even after their meticulously planned parting the pair still saw as much of each other as Queen's hectic touring and recording schedule permitted. Freddie owed this woman so much, and henceforth his generosity towards her would be boundless and, as much as was possible, kept from the media. He and Mary had decided upon having their own space while Queen had been touring. 'I'd been living in the same little Kensington flat for ages,' he told James Johnson of the *Evening Standard*, 'So I phoned Mary, my girlfriend, from America and asked her to find us a place.'

Freddie had recently relocated to another flat in Stafford Terrace, but when Mary sent him photographs of Garden Lodge, a huge Georgian mansion in Kensington's Logan Place, set in a quarter-acre of semi-landscaped garden, yet all tucked clandestinely behind a ten-foot wall, he at once authorized her to purchase it—the asking price was a cool £500,000. At the same time, he bought a luxury apartment for Mary, and for the umpteenth time tried to persuade his parents to let him buy them a more substantial property than the modest Feltham semi they had occupied since 1964. Stubbornly they refused his generosity yet again, knowing how much this hurt his feelings. Rusi Dalal, a Parsee spokesman and friend of the Bulsaras, later explained their predicament: 'Freddie's parents were unhappy about his homosexuality. Being gay is not accepted in our religion, which as we have so few believers can only be passed on from a father to his children—well, there lies the problem.'

Garden Lodge had been built as a vastly extended artist's studio for the Hoares, a family of wealthy merchant bankers, and

Freddie of course could never resist referring to his new home as 'The Hoare House', though he did surprise friends by announcing that, for the time being at least, he would not be moving in, saying, 'Why should I, when I have a nice, comfortable flat?'

Freddie did begin an extremely costly four-year restoration programme on Garden Lodge, transforming a characterless, musty old house into a warm, breathing palatial residence with eight bedrooms, four bathrooms, a multi-mirrored dressing-room, and even a minstrels' gallery—causing it to be dubbed 'The Graceland of Glam Rock' by one visiting reporter. Three rooms on the upper floor were knocked into one to form Freddie's bedroom, and he added a domed, illuminated roof which created any number of special 'mood' effects. His emperor bed was so heavy that it had to be hoisted up to the room by crane, and the electronic gadgets for this room alone are said to have cost in excess of £30,000.

Garden Lodge may have been Freddie's intended topic of conversation during his interview with the *Evening Standard*, which was conducted on the eve of Queen's free concert at Hyde Park. Sadly, this was a time when most journalists were only really interested in the 'Is-He-Or-Isn't-He?' aspect of his persona, particularly when he turned up, as he did for this interview, clad in a white satin ensemble—so tight around the middle that he had to unbutton the top of his trousers to sit down -- and with the fingernails of one hand painted black. Even so, while over-camping every anecdote and gesture, like Marc Bolan and the New York Dolls' Johnny Thunders, he was able to pass himself off successfully as a heterosexual trapped inside a hugely extroverted glam rock exterior.

An example of Freddie's fooling of the media occurred when James Johnson asked him if he and Mary would ever get around to tying the knot. There was no hint that such a union would not take place, but an almost inspiring, 'Though we are very close, I don't really see us getting married for a while. Marriage is the kind of responsibility I don't want at this stage of my career.' All of which enabled Johnson to draw the conclusion which Freddie had manipulated: 'The whirlwind of success that Queen's exotic singer has become caught up in is such that there is no longer time for the niceties of life, like house-hunting or getting married.'

Some years later, when their split had long been public knowledge, Mary told the press, 'The more I knew Freddie, the more I grew to love him. You don't need a piece of paper to be married. *Our* marriage was in the heart.' After his death, however, she would be a little more forthcoming, telling his journalist friend David Wigg that she would have felt jealous had Freddie been having heterosexual relationships, but that she could never feel so about something she could never understand. 'I realized that I couldn't have him physically any more, but I could go on loving him mentally,' she explained, 'I was strong enough to accept that he was bisexual or gay, and it never stopped me loving him. I never saw his boyfriends as a threat.'

Now, Freddie joked about how Mary had complained at his having an upright piano next to the bed—so that he could compose in the middle of the night, if need be—adding more seriously:

> All my lovers have asked me why they couldn't replace Mary. She's the only true friend I have, and I don't want anybody else. To me, she was my common-law wife. To me, it was marriage. I couldn't fall in love with a man the way I did with Mary, and I'll love her until I draw my last breath.

During the first two days of September 1976, Queen participated in the Scottish Festival of Popular Music, by giving two concerts at the recently refurbished Edinburgh Playhouse. Ten days later, they played an open-air show at Cardiff castle in near-torrential rain without a single fan leaving the venue. And on 18 September—the sixth anniversary of Jimi Hendrix's death—their legendary free concert took place in London's Hyde Park.

The concert was billed as Queen's way of expressing their gratitude towards their British fans for supporting them over the past few years. By and large it had been orchestrated by Richard Branson, the founder of Virgin Records, not an easy task, for the conditions laid down by the Park authorities were stringent: exact start and finish times with no running over, no alcohol whatsoever, and the strictest security. Even the group were not allowed to arrive at the venue in their own cars. In full stage-gear they were smuggled through the gates in the back of a laundry van for what would be Hyde Park's biggest pop event since the Rolling Stones' eulogy to Brian Jones, their drowned drummer, seven years previously.

Not everyone, however, was confident of Queen's success. Harry Doherty, a journalist who had described their Edinburgh concerts as the best he had ever attended, told French rock magazine *More*, 'In spite of their obvious talent, I'm not at all convinced they will pull this thing off. It's too big, for one thing. Secondly, Queen are not yet important enough. They'll end up a laughing stock!'

Doherty was proved wrong by an estimated 20,000 fans, considerably more than had turned up for the Stones, who flocked to the venue to persevere with support acts Supercharge, Steve Hillage and Kiki Dee. 'It would be *too* complimentary of me to describe *any* of them as better than mediocre,' Doherty observed, before cheering Freddie as he strutted on to the stage to the strains of 'Procession', wearing a white leotard. 'Welcome to our picnic by the Serpentine,' he piped, before launching into 'Keep Yourself Alive'. Later in the show, he wore a black leotard complete with diamanté codpiece—but there would be no encore, in spite of the massive roar of approval which went up after each song, particularly the newly composed 'Tie Your Mother Down', and Freddie's plaintive 'You Take My Breath Away', which he sang alone, accompanying himself on the piano. The concert was being broadcast live, by Kenny Everett on Capital Radio, and filmed for inclusion in a Queen documentary to be transmitted later by the BBC, therefore the police were taking no chances. Freddie had been instructed that, should he so much as step on to the stage after the group's allotted 100-minute slot, he personally would be held responsible and arrested. In fact, this would not have been possible as, on the dot, the power was switched off—and even the crowd had to make their way out of Hyde Park in almost total darkness.

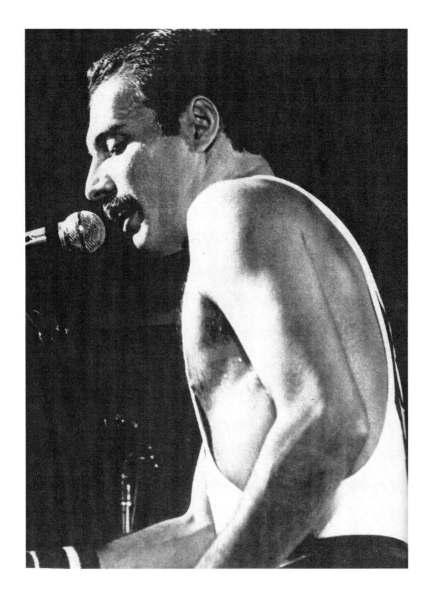

'In the wake of the human tornado.' (Bret/Cinemago, Paris)

Four: A Marvel Of Grace!

For Queen, one triumph followed another: two hit singles in Britain and the United States ('You're My Best Friend' and the gospel-like 'Somebody To Love'), and an album which reached Number One in Britain and Number 5 in America. *A Day At The Races*, so named after another Marx Brothers comedy film, was released with a fanfare of publicity on 10 December 1976. The press launch took place six days later at Kempton Park, when one of the races on the card was sponsored in its honour and won by John Francome on Lanzarote. And *still* the group was elated by the music press. 'Too formulated, too smartass, too reliant on trickery as a substitute for inspiration,' opined *Sounds*.

On 1 December, Queen inadvertently helped to create a slice of television history when work commitments forced them into the eleventh-hour cancellation of an appearance on Bill Grundy's television chat show, *Today*. EMI were asked to supply an alternative, and chose their latest punk acquisition, the Sex Pistols, without any doubt the most hyped, controversial and arguably talentless act of their day. In what must have been the most humiliating moment of his career, Grundy sat through the interview, unable to stop the tirade of filthy language and atrocious behaviour which brought so many complaints from viewers that the Sex Pistols were dropped by EMI, and Grundy, the innocent bystander, found himself fired.

At the end of the year, the Queen Fan Club issued its first 'biography' of the group. This was little more than a pamphlet, but contained a number of excellent photographs, four stunning portraits of the individual members of the group, a list of all their award and appearances to date, and individual questionnaires. Thus fans were able to learn that Brian May liked Natalie Wood but hated Johnny Mathis, that John Deacon's favourite magazine was *Men Only*, and that Roger Taylor hated '98 per cent of music recorded today'. Some of Freddie's responses, of course, were typically outrageous:

* Hair/Eyes: Midnight black/liquid brown.
* Favourite Movies: Anything with Mae West.
* Favourite Food: Nectar.
* Favourite Drink: Champagne in a glass slipper.
* What were you doing before you started playing professionally?: A Kensington poseur.
* Your dream?: To remain the divine, lush creature that I am.
* Special talent other than music: Poncing and poovery.

On 13 January 1977, in sub-zero temperatures, Queen began a 40-plus-date tour of the United States at the Milwaukee Auditorium, initially supported by now-forgotten bands Head East and Cheap Trick, then by the Irish group Thin Lizzy. In an attempt to capitalize on the Queen's Silver Jubilee in June, the promoters billed it 'The Queen Lizzy Tour'!

In America, 'Bohemian Rhapsody' was performed in its entirety for the first time—the multi-dubbed, 180-strong vocal section being replaced by a backing tape and a fireworks display while the group took a curtain-call. During the early days of the tour, however, the group were subjected to a vicious smear campaign from the US music press, who momentarily were almost as deliberately oblivious to Queen's talents as their British counterpart. Everything they performed, said and did, their appearance and personal lives, was denounced in the most vitriolic manner, whereas Thin Lizzy were praised beyond belief even by critics who were not present during their concerts. The ruse backfired when many thousands of rock enthusiasts who were fans of neither group flocked to venues out of sheer curiosity—only to come away as confirmed Queen addicts.

While in Los Angeles for two shows at the Forum on 3 and 4 March, Queen received a summons from Groucho Marx, who invited them to tea at his Hollywood home. The press temporarily shelved their attacks. If Groucho could rave over this bunch of English extroverts, then so could they, for the moment, so as not to offend one of their national institutions. They flocked to Beverly Hills to witness this most extraordinary scene. The elderly comic, in the last year of his life, had already sent the group a telegram congratulating them on the success of *A Night At The Opera*, and he was now photographed wearing the *Queen II* tour jacket they had given him, along with an honorary engraved gold disc. There was also an impromptu recital when Groucho crooned a couple of his old film hits, and Queen sang Brian May's '39', *a capella*, in his living-room.

Back in England, Queen were still being hounded by the music press, though this time there was consolation in that they were not alone. Led Zeppelin, Genesis and The Who were declared 'has-beens' in the wake of the punk explosion, and when Queen's single, 'Tie Your Mother Down', stalled at Number 31 in the charts, the death-knell was duly sounded. The fact that Queen stood for everything that this sudden this cacophany of vulgarity did not—melody, comprehensible lyrics, good taste, manners and sensibility—counted for little with many rock journalists. Nor did Freddie's habit of toasting audiences with champagne and quips like, 'People want art. They want showbiz. They *want* to see you rush off in your limousine!'

This latter statement formed the basis for Freddie's interview with Tony Stewart of the *New Musical Express*, a meeting peppered with expletives and bitchy asides. The meeting was arranged by Freddie's new personal manager Paul Prenter, a 26-year-old Irishman who had been brought in by John Reid and who, though a good friend at the time, would cause Freddie much grief in the future.

Exactly why Freddie agreed to such an interview is not known, bearing in mind that neither man could stand the sight of the other. It may well be that his sole intention was to avenge himself and Queen for the spite inflicted upon them by the music press over the last few years, and in particular this journalist who had already dismissed Freddie as 'A rock 'n' roll spiv who uses his band as a vehicle for an elaborate exhibition of narcissism.' If so, it almost worked. Freddie did his utmost to make Stewart feel ill at ease, insisting that his burly bodyguard be present throughout the interview, and intimidating him at every opportunity. 'Seemingly he is determined that I should feel subordinate to him,' Stewart observed.

The bitching began within minutes, when Freddie told his antagonist, 'Darling, if everything you read in the press about me was true, I wouldn't be sitting here talking to you today. I'd be too worried about my ego!' Then, adding that he was living life to the full he cracked, 'I hope that when *you* better yourself in your position you'll enjoy yourself too!' When Stewart criticized Queen for their stagewear and glitzy performances, Freddie hit back with a tarty, 'What do *you* know about show business? Can you imagine doing the sort of things we've written, like "Rhapsody" and "Somebody To Love" in jeans, with absolutely no presentation?'

Stewart certainly gave the impression that he knew little about culture when, discussing Freddie's proposed tribute to the great Russian ballet dancer, Nijinsky, he suggested that most rock fans would like himself think that Nijinsky was the famous racehorse, adding that in any case he was unqualified to review ballet. At this Freddie hit back with a sarcastic, 'What makes you think you're qualified to do rock 'n' roll?' The real venom surfaced when inevitable comparisons were made between the British and American music press. 'The Americans don't have the same kind of prejudices,' Freddie observed scathingly. 'If they can do it why the fuck can't people over here? You're too narrow-minded. You're the bloody arrogant sods that just don't want to learn. You don't want to be told *anything*. You feel you know it all before it's even happened!'

Tony Stewart exacted his revenge by heading his feature, 'Is This Man A Prat?', and by insulting Freddie's intelligence by adding asides which the singer deemed 'pig-ignorant', such as, 'If ever I see Margot Fonteyn down the Rainbow, I'll buy her a pint!' Freddie was further incensed by Stewart's gratuitous comment, 'His fingers were vigorously pruning his hair, as if in search of nits.' Worse still was the acid observation, 'In this iconoclastic atmosphere there is nothing more redundant, or meaningless, than a posturing ballerina toasting the audience, as Mercury does, with "May you all have champagne for breakfast!"' Freddie swore that he would never speak to the music press again.

Queen returned home early in March, though there was little time for resting up before leaving for Stockholm, early in May, to begin a brief European tour. Here, Freddie wore his infamous 'L'Apres-Midi d'un Faune' costume for the first time. The idea had been devised by Nijinsky himself for the Ballet Russes in 1912, and revised by Rudolph Valentino a decade later. Freddie copied it to the last detail, raising more than a few eyebrows among the clutch of reporters gathered backstage at the Ice Stadium—who were unable to avert their gaze from his crotch—by quipping, 'It's all me, darlings. I don't have my socks down there, or any coke bottle!' He then leapt on to the stage, executed a few pirouettes, and the audience went wild!

Writing his review of the show, one these journalists drew a comparison between Freddie and his current alter-image by applying to Freddie, the star, what Jean Cocteau had written about Nijinsky, the man: 'On one side of the curtain he was a marvel of grace, on the other an extraordinary example of strength and weakness...'

Queen lost count of the accolades they received during this European tour, which culminated in a superb concert at the Basle Sporthalle on 19 May. Two evenings previously at a boat party following their show at the Ahoy Hall in Rotterdam, they had been presented with an astonishing 35 silver, gold and platinum discs for record sales in Holland alone.

Flamboyance was the order of the day when Queen arrived back in Britain for a tour which concluded with two shows at London's Earls Court on 6 and 7 June. A banner, emblazoned with the announcement QUEEN IN CONCERT, was hung from the front of the building and sparked off the silliest of rows between the Mayor of Hammersmith and John Reid. Upon seeing this the Mayor actually believed that *the* Queen had been booked to make a personal appearance as part of the borough's Jubilee celebrations, and that someone had forgotten to tell him! What happened next, however, was even more ridiculous, for an official from the Mayor's office actually contacted Buckingham Palace and requested an explanation. Then, having learned the truth, the Mayor made an even bigger fool of himself by telephoning John Reid and demanding that the sign be taken down because it might confuse the public. It was in fact Freddie who responded on Reid's behalf, saying, 'Tell him I'll take it down myself, dear, and throttle the silly little man with it!'

At Earls Court, Queen proudly unveiled their new 'baby' —a 5,000-pound lighting-rig, shaped like a crown and measuring 54 x 26 feet, which rose slowly from the stage, exposing the group in a dazzling extravaganza of flashing beams. Over the next few years there would be several such crowns custom built for travelling, but this first one was the best and most expensive—setting the group back a cool £50,000. And at the end of each concert thousands of red, white and blue balloons were released into the audience to commemorate the Queen's Silver Jubilee.

The music press attacked Queen this time for their 'pointless extravagance', and even had a dig at their music, mindless of the fact that the 36,000 tickets had sold in record time. What they did not mention was that the group had donated the proceeds from their second show plus the collection from a post-gig party held in a marquee in Holland Park—an alleged £100,000—to the Jubilee Fund.

Queen's reverence and patriotism were a far cry from the disgraceful behaviour of their 'rivals' the Sex Pistols—for while there were mass street-parties and pageantries throughout Britain and the Commonwealth, their highly offensive 'God Save The Queen' burst into the Top Ten and their manager, Malcolm Mclaren, hosted a boat-party on the Thames which was attended by hundreds of fans sporting T-shirts depicting their sovereign wearing a safety-pin through her nose. A few weeks later, while Queen were working on their new album and the Sex Pistols were in an adjacent studio recording their *Never Mind The Bollocks* album, Freddie bumped into their frontman, Sid Vicious, a thoroughly unpleasant, virulently homophobic individual who could not stand him. Freddie had the last word, however, when Vicious—referring to the Nijinsky costume –pronounced sarcastically in front of reporters, 'So, you're really brought ballet to the masses, then?' To which Freddie replied, quick as a flash, 'Ah, Mr Ferocious. Well, we're trying our best, dear!'

Extravagance was the order of the day on 5 September 1977 when Freddie celebrated his 31st birthday at Cherry Brown's 'hip' Country Cousin Restaurant in London's fashionable King's Road. The sumptuous bash was organised by his lover David Minns, who later confessed that the most expensive items on the bill were not the food and drink, but the thousands of flowers which decorated the establishment from top to bottom. Freddie had insisted on orchids, even for the toilets.

71

Each of the 150 invitations was handwritten by Freddie and bore the inscription, 'Dress to kill!' The guest list, a veritable Who's Who of the famous and infamous, also included just about every record company big-wig in England, some of whom were used to outrageous and frequently despicable behaviour from their clients. Even so, the slapstick antics of Elton John and Freddie's pal Kenny Everett were tame compared with those of the American female impersonator, Divine, another great star who died far too young. Freddie followed Divine's disco and film career with avid interest, and told a French reporter after his friend had been awarded the nickname, 'The Filthiest Person Alive", 'Anyone who can eat *real* dog-shit, dear, simply *has* to be a legend!' Now, the 340-pound, mini-skirted actor put on a show of his own. Ordering the near-naked snake-charmer hired by Minns as part of the evening's entertainment to lie on top of a table, legs akimbo, he barked, 'And now, honey, for the orgasm of a lifetime!'—before 'ejaculating' the entire contents of a magnum of champage across her body. Freddie thanked him with a chirpy, 'Thanks, Divi. I'm so glad you could *come!*'

The hilarity aside, however, Freddie's relationship with Minns was falling apart at the seams, and would only deteriorate further the higher his particular star ascended. Like Mary Austin and several others, Minns could not accept taking a backseat while his lover was sleeping around indiscriminately. 'I couldn't hate him,' he observes in the book he co-authored with David Evans, 'Yet neither did I kid myself that we would ever be best friends again. Our close friendship was a closed chapter.'

According to Paul Prenter, the relationship ended soon afterwards during a trip to Miami, after Freddie made eyes at a hunky young American dancer named Dane Clark, who had once worked as Elton John's assistant and dresser. 'Minns screamed at Freddie, calling him a "faceless hussy",' Prenter recalled, explaining how in the hotel lift Minns had begun bashing Freddie over the head with a shoe, only to be smacked in the teeth. The singer, apparently undaunted, had then gone off to the beach with his latest 'catch', whom he had subsequently hired as his own dresser, a position Clark retained until 1982.

Other friends have also spoken of how they were compelled to keep a more suitable distance as the potentially lethal combination of artistic temperament and fame began taking its toll, fuelled by those faithful allies of the *monstre sacré*: sex, drink, drugs and an acute neurasthenia brought on by the seemingly unsuccessful, interminable search for Mr Perfect. Freddie's behaviour caused problems for the group, though not for John Reid as has been suggested. As David Evans explained:

> Queen and John Reid got together precisely because Freddie was gay. They were two gay men, working very well together. The three boys, however, always felt uncomfortable with Freddie's gayness. They weren't scared of it, just apprehensive. They didn't know how to handle it.

Following the relative failure of their last single, Queen had released their first EP, *Good Old Fashioned Lover Boy*, which had only reached Number 17 in the charts, while Roger's debut single, 'I Wanna Testify', had bombed completely. Brian's venture with Lonnie Donegan—playing on two tracks of the skiffle star's comeback album, *Putting On The Style*—had fared slightly better, though these solo projects only pushed the tabloids into fabricating rumours that the group were about to split because they were incapable of coping with the competition from the punk invasion.

Queen's 'problem' was effectively solved by the October release of Freddie's 'We Are The Champions' c/w 'Brian's equally anthemic 'We Will Rock You', a song which was considered just as important as the A-side, resulting in both numbers receiving equal air-play in Britain, where the record reached Number 2 in the charts, and in the United States where it peaked at Number 4, Queen's biggest hit there so far. 'We Will Rock You' became the anthem of the New York Yankees, whereas 'We Are The Champions' remains possibly the most played of all Queen's songs, and is regularly chanted on the terraces by football supporters worldwide, besides being included in television fitness and strength contests such as *Gladiators* and *The Krypton Factor*. 'It's the most egotistical and arrogant song I've ever written,' Freddie said. The video, directed by Derek Burbridge, was filmed at the New London Theatre—Freddie's choice, for it was here in 1972 that one of his idols, Marlene Dietrich, had filmed her one and only television spectacular—and instead of hiring extras to make up an audience, fans were brought in from all over England. After the shoot, as a token of their appreciation, Queen treated them to a complimentary concert.

A few days later, Queen were able to sever their ties with Trident, buying out their one per cent royalties' clause in their termination contract. It also emerged that they were experiencing difficulties with their current manager, John Reid, largely because Reid could not handle Elton John *and* one of the world's biggest bands, while offering both his undivided attention. The severance contract, negotiated by Jim Beach and signed with typical aplomb in the back of Freddie's Rolls-Royce, affected a break which was expedient and amicable, but costly. Henceforth, Reid would exact a hefty 15 per cent royalty on all the albums Queen had released so far, along with an undisclosed, allegedly massive cash settlement—enough of a 'penalty' for the group to opt for self-management from now on.

Over the ensuing months, three limited companies were set up: Queen Productions, Queen Music, and Queen Films. Advised on complex tax issues by their accountant, the group also formed

Rainbow Productions to handle their overseas revenue which, they were told, would be exempt from British tax so long as they spent no more than sixty-five days of each year in England. They were also advised to record sections of their albums in different countries to avoid paying performance taxes, which of course saved them a fortune. In their first 'year out', as it is technically known, each member of the group awarded himself a salary of £700,000—enough for anyone to retire on, as one journalist ridiculously suggested to Freddie, who typically quipped, 'Retire, dear? But what else could I do? I can't cook, and I'm not a very good housewife. I'm just a musical prostitute, dear!'

The group were now able to afford a few luxuries, such as the huge lacquered Japanese piano which Freddie bought in New York, and the private plane Queen hired to commute between venues on their next American tour—which opened in Portland on 11 November 1977, a few days after the release of their *News Of The World* album.

Reaching the Top Five on both sides of the Atlantic and selling 7 million copies worldwide, the album had a sci-fi cover designed by Frank Kelly Freas—an adaptation of a magazine cover he had drawn during the Fifties which depicted the corpses of Freddie and Brian in the clutches of an enormous robot, while Roger and John tumble lifelessly into space. *News Of The World* was probably their rowdiest, most sensational variation of musical styles so far, though only three of its eleven songs were written by Freddie. The title was, of course, a direct reference to the tabloid attacks of the last few years. The group actually met Freas in Norfolk, Virginia, where they were appearing at the Scope Arena, and where the Chrysler Museum was holding an exhibition of his work.

For Freddie, however, nothing surpassed his meeting, on 2 December, with Liza Minelli. Judy Garland's daughter was appearing on Broadway in *The Act*—and Freddie was apparently too shy to ask to meet her after the show. This was rectified after the second of Queen's two concerts at the Madison Square Garden, where Minelli asked to see *him*. On this particular occasion he had received a roisterous welcome by strutting on to the stage wearing a Yankees' baseball strip.

During this tour, the American music press afforded the group respect. Only one concert was not played to a capacity crowd, the one in Dayton, Ohio, on 4 December, when adverse weather conditions prevented many fans from getting to the venue—and when it was revealed that the auditorium at the university had a half-inch coating of frost because of a heating failure. Even so, the show went ahead and no one was disappointed. Queen's most extravagant performance, Freddie's way of giving fans a good time, took place at the Los Angeles Forum three days before Christmas. At the end of the show, a security man stomped on to the stage dressed as Santa Claus—flanked by friends and members of Queen's entourage dressed as Christmas trees, gingerbreadmen, clowns and reindeers—carrying a large sack, out of which popped Freddie to direct the audience through several raucous choruses of 'White Christmas', while fake snow, glitter and pink balloons cascaded from the rafters. To show there were no hard feelings, their ex-manager John Reid danced around the stage dressed a pixie. Yet despite the success of their US tour, Queen's next single released there—Brian May's 'It's Late' –was an almost total flop and their next British single, John Deacon's 'Spread Your Wings', released on the eve of their European tour, only made it to the lower reaches of the Top Forty.

Europe, thankfully, was another story. Queen were first popular entertainers to play two consecutive concerts the Foret Nationale de Bruxelles and be invited back for a third within the week. On 23/24 April they played the Pavilion de Paris, renowned for its tetchy, hard-to-please audiences, and received an unprecedented standing ovation. On 28 April they played the

Berliner Deutschlandhalle, and after the show were escorted to a notorious transvestite club, Chez Patachou (*not* to be confused with the famous, respectable Parisian nightspot run by the equally famous *chanteuse* of the same name, of whom Freddie was also a fan), where the resident dance troupe performed several of their songs in a crude Weimar sketch that even Freddie found surprising. The next day, Brian and Roger crossed Checkpoint Charlie into the city's Eastern sector, while John did some sightseeing and Freddie stayed in his hotel room with a German 'friend', and cracked, 'If they get *me* over there, dear, they'll never let me out!'

Returning to England early in May, Queen played just five gigs at two venues—Stafford's Bingley Hall, and London's Empire Pool. They had already outlined most of the tracks on their next album, *Jazz*—their first to be recorded outside Britain—and while Roger and John flew to Switzerland to work on what they had so far at the Mountain Studios, Montreux, Brian stayed put for the birth of his first son, James, in June, before flying with his family to Canada.

Freddie, probably putting his failed project with Eddie Howell down to a bad experience, lingered long enough in England to complete a venture with another friend, the actor-singer Peter Straker, who had appeared in the controversial stage-show *Hair*, and was about to cut an album. 'He was a perfectionist,' Straker recalled. 'His inventiveness, coupled with a meticulous attention to detail, brought me enormous satisfaction. Freddie celebrated his achievements with extravagant and sumptuous gestures, executed with enormous kindness.' Freddie's generosity in this instance was to invest £20,000 of his own money in *This One's On Me*, which EMI released in 1978. But though he put a lot of energy into promoting the album, enthusing about Straker's "finely-tuned" voice, the album was not the success he had anticipated.

At the end of July 1978, Freddie was working with the rest of the group in Montreux when a photograph appeared in a French magazine of him swinging from a chandelier at Roger Taylor's 29th birthday party. This was a pretty tame affair compared with Freddie's own birthday bash, two months later in Nice, where there was a limitless supply of exotic food, drink and cocaine and where at the end of the evening everyone but Freddie, the voyeur, stripped off and dived into the hotel pool. It was while they were in Nice that Freddie took an active interest in that year's Tour de France, which passed along the Cote d'Azur—or more specifically, in a young cyclist named Charles who had dropped out of the race with a ham-string injury, and who subsequently spent the night with him. It was this exciting experience which inspired Freddie to compose 'Bicycle Race', which Queen decided at once would be their next single. Charles told me, 'Watching the Tour de France go zipping by, Freddie observed how much more exciting the event would have been, had all those muscular young hunks been naked, or at least wearing just jock-straps. He told me what a wonderful video *that* would have made!'

To an extent, Freddie's dream was partially realized when Queen's production company accepted his proposition to hire sixty-five female models to engage in a nude cycle race around Wimbledon Stadium for the promotional video. This was shot under 'very tight security'—though not tight enough to prevent a paparazzi invasion—at a cost of £20,000 on 17 September, by which time Brian May had supplied the very appropriate 'Fat Bottomed Girls' for the double A-side scheduled for release the following month. The bicycles were supplied free by Halfords, who sent Queen Productions a bill for the seats, which had had to be destroyed.

The single, featuring a 'bum-shot' of the winning girl, brought screams of protest from moralists, forcing it to be withdraw from the shops, until the offending posterior had been clothed in a pair of drawn-on black panties. The music press hated and condemned both songs, the *New Musical Express* going so far as to arrogantly publish a rear-view of Freddie with the caption, 'Fat-Bottomed Queen'. Even so, it reached Number 11 in the charts, by which time Queen were in the middle of another turbulent sell-out tour of the United States.

The tour kicked off in Dallas on 28 September 1978, and sitting in the audience was Merrill Shindler of *Playgirl*. The 'entertainment for women' magazine had recently published full-frontal shots of Fifties' pop-idol Fabian, along with nude pictures of several top actors, sportsmen, and policitians—and rather hoped that Freddie might enhance their gallery with a centrefold. For a man for whom blatant exhibitionism was second nature, however, this was going too far. Shindler described the curtain-call:

> Mercury is the sort of performer who attracts and repels at the same time—sort of like a rock Wayne Newton. On stage he minces and prances about like an epicine Crusader Rabbit—strutting and striking the most outlandish poses in crotch-bulging sequined tights, then waggling the microphone stand between his thighs and dropping bons mots like, 'I'm going to take a little rest now—maybe get a blowjob backstage!' Just who will be administering that blowjob is anybody's guess, since Freddie is quite willing to explain, 'I'll go to bed with anything—one sex is as good as another.' But for those who might be offended that Mercury is only in rock 'n' roll for the perversity open to him, he also adds, 'My object in life is to make a lot of money and spend it, though these days I tend to spend it before I make it!'

Three days later in New Orleans—a Hallowe'en few of Queen's entourage or the assembled guests would live down for some time—a pre-launch party for *Jazz* was held in the Imperial Room at the plush Fairmount Hotel. Record company executives were invited from England, France, Germany and the United States—all sharing a mutual financial interest in the group, but most of them meeting for the first time. Among the 400 guests were representatives of the world's press who reported the events of the midnight-till-dawn extravaganza with gusto—most of them coming away from the Fairmount knowing little more about the new album than when they had arrived, but all having participated in the wildest rock party of the year: fire-eaters, exotic dancers and hermaphrodite strippers, dwarfs, naked female mud-wrestlers, Zulu tribesmen and contortionists. Freddie also supplied several 'models' of both sexes, who spent the entire six hours of the party on their knees in a back-room, entertaining the record company executives and some of his friends who had not 'scored' in the conventional way. He told a young female reporter, who looked innocent enough when entering the Fairmount and anything but when leaving, 'Most hotels offer their clients room-service, dear. This one provides *lip*-service!'

Merrill Shindler, describing the bash as 'a Saturday night in Sodom', nevertheless took great delight in dictating a running commentary of events for *Playgirl*—only to have the ensuing feature heavily censored by the editor. It concluded:

> 25-cent piece, and stuffed with twenty-dollar bills. There are drag queens in slingbacks and bouffants, and a bevvy of 300-pound Samoan women— On the tabletop in front of me is a painfully thin young woman whose sole item of dress is a G-string not much bigger than a naked as jaybirds—one of whom has mastered the knack of puffing a cigarette with her vagina. Queen's latest album

80

is called Jazz, though there is no jazz on it. As Freddie points out, 'Jazz can mean anything from bullshit to jive to music!' And, by the time you read this column, it will have sold over a million copies, maybe two. And now, back to Queen's party at the Fairmount Hotel. It's a gala affair, an infectious event. So infectious that one guest at the next table decides to take off her dress and join the strippers on the tabletops...

If the parents of younger, more impressionable Queen fans read any of these reviews, some even more explicit than Merrill Shindler's, they could hardly ignore the album itself, for it came with a complimentary poster of the naked bicycle girls. This caused few problems in Britain, but in the American Bible Belt there was such a furore that the album was deemed *pornographic*, and banned until the package had been redesigned to incorporate an application form so that fans could send for the poster by mail order. Freddie then decided to give these moralists something to complain about—for Queen's 16 and 17 November concerts at New York's Madison Square Garden, he hired twenty naked women to cycle back and forth across the stage.

There were further problems when a religious group threatened Elektra with legal action over one of the sleeve credits, which read, 'Thunderbolt Courtesy Of God'. This amounted to nothing, however, when Brian May explained that he had stood out in the street in Montreux to tape a thunderstorm which had then been incorporated into the ending of 'Dead On Time'. And the controversy naturally only enhanced sales: *Jazz* reached Number 6 in the *Billboard* album chart, and Number 2 in Britain.

Scorpio Rising (Redferns)

Five: It's All In The Game

In January 1979, Queen flew to Hamburg to begin their longest tour so far—twenty-eight concerts, including off-circuit towns and cities such as Saarbrucken and Poitiers, and two dates in Yugoslavia. Much of the time Freddie wore an excruciatingly tight harlequin costume, and on one occasion had just performed 'Love Of My Life' when Chris Taylor, Roger's (straight) roadie walked on to the stage to hand him his maraccas and a glass of water. Freddie introduced him to the 12,000 fans with, 'This is Crystal. He's got a big dick, and he's good in bed!' On another, he closed the proceedings with, 'Thank you, God bless, and sweet dreams—you lot of tarts!'

The tour ended with three shows at the Pavilion de Paris. By now some of Queen's British camp followers—Freddie called them the Royal Family—had begun tinkling bicycle bells as a means of requesting the two bicycle numbers, and for some reason this irked French fans, who tolerated the practice until halfway through the third show, when they began fighting. When several of Queen's road crew joined in the fracas, the local *gendarmerie* alerted the riot-squad, who invaded the venue with batons and tear-gas.

At the time of the tour, Queen were shortlisted to compose the score for the comic-strip adventure film, *Flash Gordon*. The Italian-born producer, Dino de Laurentis, was dubious about taking them on, barking impatiently at a meeting with his backers, 'Queen? Never heard of 'em. Who the hell are *they*?' Persuaded to listen to *A Night At The Opera*, however, de Laurentis very quickly agreed to a commission.

Freddie was in his element, working and improvising in front of a giant screen while the eponymous hero, played by Sam J Jones, flexed, preened and swashbuckled towards victory in high-camp fashion. 'Relentlessly smirky, decadent and homoerotic,' enthused Paul Roen in his book, *High Camp: A Gay Guide To Camp & Cult Films*. 'It's extremely gay, mainly due to the costuming, or in some case the *lack* of costuming, and combines the dregs of Seventies disco culture with the chauvinistic cruelty of Reaganism.' Famed British film critic Barry Norman observed, 'Great fun, providing you ignore the plot and concentrate on the corny performances and cheesy special effects.'

Neither did it go unobserved that Jones—an ethereal-looking, dyed-blond, muscular six-footer—had first gained recognition when he had bared his considerable assets for a *Playgirl* centrefold. Subsequently, when he learned that four years earlier Dino de Laurentis had directed an emotive remake of the classic horror movie, *King Kong*—one which had been panned by the critics—Freddie told a friend, 'Dino made *King Kong*. Now it's my greatest ambition to make it with King Dong!' His plans were scuppered, however, when one of Sam J Jones' pals informed him that the actor was 'not that way inclined'.

Each of Queen's 1979 concerts was taped to enable the edited, remixed highlights to be incorporated into the double album, *Live Killers*, which was pieced together at Musicland Studios, in Munich. Released in June, it peaked at Number 3 in the charts, surprising the group's record company, for by this time the market was flooded with bootleg tapes, many of them of equal if not better quality than this one—which had also been publicly condemned by Roger Taylor. At around this time, too, Queen bought Mountain Studios, situated on the shores of the picturesque Lake Geneva—a strange move, for in these early, reckless years Freddie often claimed that he could not stand the tranquility, declaring that the studio should have been *under* the lake, rather than next to it.

In April, Queen flew to Japan to an even more riotous welcome than their first, four years earlier: as with Europe, there

84

were off-the-circuit concerts in Kanazawa and Sapporo. Also, this time the Japanese had an 'anthem' of their own. 'Teo Toriatte (Let Us Cling Together)' written by Brian for inclusion in *A Day At The Races*, had a chorus which the group sang in Japanese. By now, however, Freddie was beginning to tire of these mostly teenage fans who reacted hysterically to each and every song, so much so that much of what was happening on the stage was deafened by their screeching. 'There used to be a time when I loved all this teenybop screaming,' Freddie complained, 'But now I think I would prefer them to *listen* what we're playing.'

Then it was back to Mountain Studios, where Queen began working on their new album which, in effect, would not be released until the following summer. For Freddie, this was a period of considerable contentment. He loved working with the irascible German engineer, Reinhardt Mack, so much so that Mack was soon being credited as 'co-producer', and henceforth would play a vital role in the Queen empire now that the group had dispensed with the services of the hitherto 'indispensable' Roy Thomas Baker.

Freddie fell for Munich in a big way, and for several years the city became his second home. Since his first visit to Germany in 1973, he had admired the country's liberated attitude towards homosexuality and the opportunity this had given him to explore a budding sexuality which was now in full, decadent bloom. Like post-Stonewall New York, Munich in the Seventies was a hotbed of gay culture where one could sample openly the delights of a wide range of clubs, cinemas, cafés and bars, without fear of disapproval or criticism from the so-called straight society. Freddie's nocturnal pilgrimages into the area known as the Bermuda Triangle often saw him accompanied by friends—Paul Prenter, Joe 'Liza' Fanelli, and Peter 'Phoebe' Freestone. Afterwards there would be wild parties in Roger Taylor's hotel suite—the 'HH', or 'Heterosexual Hangout'—and wilder ones in the suite Freddie was sharing with his pals—the 'PPP', or 'Presidential Pouffes' Parlour'.

Casting what few inhibitions he had to the wind, Freddie did exactly what he liked, where and when the mood took him. He was justifiably proud of the photograph which appeared in a German gay magazine. Wearing his now famous harlequin costume, he is seen smooching on the dance-floor with a young man who is sporting an undersized silk bomber-jacket, and nothing else. It is now known that this was the legendary gay porn star, Peter Berlin.

In next to no time, Freddie was rubbing shoulders with the likes of Amanda Lear, Helmut Berger, and Rainer Werner Fassbinder, the undisputed champion of sado-masochistic sex, alcohol and drugs whose behaviour made that of his most lascivious contemporaries appear tame. Though Freddie confessed that Fassbinder was not his 'cup of char', he did admire the odd-looking director for bravely tackling the subject of homosexuality in his work, and for attracting rave reviews from critics renowned for their homophobia. He was equally fascinated by three of Fassbinder's leading ladies—his wife Ingrid Caven, Hanna Schygulla, and Barbara Valentin, known as the German Jayne Mansfield. Freddie told a German reporter, 'I love Schygulla's ice-cool acting style, and Caven's singing voice reminds me of a cross between Piaf and Dietrich. Valentin, dear, fascinates me because she's got such great tits!'

All three stars, in common with the icons they have paid tribute to over the years, had huge gay followings across Europe and were referred to by patrons of the seedy Frisco Bar, another favourite Mercury haunt, somewhat ingloriously as 'The Three Fag-Hags'. Of the three, however, it was Vienna-born Valentin (Ursula Ledersteger, 1940-2002) who attracted him the most, and their friendship developed into a close bonding not unlike the one with Mary Austin—so much so that, when they began sharing an apartment, but only as friends, rumours ran rife that Freddie was about to become 'Mr Valentin Number Four'. In fact, Valentin had only been married once, and was still married (for a few more years) to the German director, Helmut Dietl. The fact that he may have 'turned the other way' upset many of Freddie's gay fans, especially when Reinhardt Mack said in an interview that his gayness was perfectly dispensable—to the effect that he would have 'grown' out of it given an opportunity to sire children, and bearing in mind that he had always loved women! The statement has since been dismissed by Freddie's close friends and flippant and ridiculous. One told me:

> Although Freddie could have married and made a wonderful father, he was never, never a hypocrite and could never have sworn to stay faithful or change his ways. He was sublimely happy the way he was. And being gay isn't an illness. You can't suddenly decide you're cured and go from being one way to another.

Many years later, another Queen spokesperson who chose to remain anonymous told the *Daily Mirror* that Freddie only lived with the two women in his life so that his mother would not ask too many awkward questions about his sexuality—a statement which makes one wonder how, with all the scurrilous tabloid stories and Freddie's outrageous comments she could *not* have known the truth. It is also an incontestable fact that while Freddie and Barbara Valentin may have been sleeping together, this relationship was entirely different from the one with Mary Austin because they were usually sleeping on either side of some young man either or both of them had picked up at one of Munich's countless rough-trade joints.

Admitting she and Freddie often bashed each other whenever jealousy reared its ugly head—which was often, the busty actress added—'We had *exactly* the same taste in men. Our favourites were big-all-over truck-driver types. We couldn't get enough of them!' Another of his German lovers, Kurt, revealed Freddie's 'demoralization process', whereby if a man tried to act too butch in the bedroom, he would be brought down a peg or two by being assigned to the role of one of Freddie's movie heroines:

> Freddie was absolutely crazy about Gloria Swanson. I was just twenty, and didn't even know who she was. He asked me to take off all my clothes, which I did most willingly. Then he plonked this huge, old-fashioned hat on my head, a mess of smelly feathers which he said Swanson had worn in Sunset Boulevard. Then he rushed downstairs to give me my cue. He yelled cut, and I descended the staircase as he improvised a scene from What Ever Happened To Baby Jane? Then he absolutely howled with laughter. Someone told me afterwards that Freddie did this sort of thing to humiliate his lovers, but I don't think so. He was such a kind, gentle man and I would do absolutely anything, now, just to hear that wonderful laugh of his once more.

On 18 August 1979, Queen made a return trip to Saarbrucken, to top the bill at an open-air festival in the 32,000-capacity Ludwigparkstadion. This time Roger was the centre of attention as he walked on to the stage sporting green hair—the result of a last-minute bleaching attempt gone wrong. The concert was beset with technical problems from start to finish—and by the end of it, Roger's frustration got the better of him and he smashed his drum-kit to pieces.

Early in October, Queen released, 'Crazy Little Thing Called Love', one of the four songs recorded in Munich. It was bouncy rockabilly number, penned by Freddie while in his bath—and one which would not have been out of place in Elvis Presley's later repertoire. 'It isn't typical of my work,' Freddie said, ahead of the critics who would lampoon it. 'But that's only because nothing *is* typical of my work!' The record quickly reached Number 2 in the British charts—a far cry from their last single, a live version of 'Love Of My Life', which had stalled at Number 63, and it gave Queen their first Number One in the United States. The video was tremendous fun, an innocuous promotion of homoeroticism tinged with Benny Hill-style humour: a leather-clad Queen, with a brilliantined, knee-padded Freddie being forcibly dragged on to the catwalk by two muscular hunks, before being groped by a bevvy of busty lovelies in suspenders—one of which sensually blows smoke into the camera while another proceeds to rip Freddie's T-shirt from top to bottom.

When first screened on *Top of the Pops*, the video brought an unexpected outburst from Rob Halford, the lead singer with the leather-and-chains hard-rock ensemble, Judas Priest, who accused Queen of 'purloining' their image. Halford threw down the gauntlet, challenging Freddie to 'prove his machismo' by using the huge motorcycle he had straddled in the film to race him around the circuit at Brands Hatch. 'Fine,' Freddie barked, adding with reference to his next project, 'So long as the gentleman agrees to do a *pas-de-deux* with the Royal Ballet!' Needless to say, the challenge was withdrawn.

'Crazy Little Thing Called Love' was chosen by Freddie, along with 'Bohemian Rhapsody', for his special charity performance with the Royal Ballet, at the London Coliseum on 7 October. A keen ballet enthusiast, he had attended many of the company's performances and was a close friend of principal dancer Wayne Eagling. 'Sadly, not close enough,' he lamented to another friend, 'I mean, how can anyone as gorgeous as that be *straight*? Mind you, dear, I did get a peep at what goes inside those tights!'

The show was to raise funds for the Society For Handicapped

Children and Eagling and his colleague, Derek Dane, put Freddie through his paces for the two routines they had especially choreographed. It proved one of the toughest ordeals of his career so far but, wearing a silver-spangled all-in-on open at the front to expose the now obligatory dense expense of chest hair, he performed each step perfectly, receiving a roisterous standing ovation from hundreds of ballet afficionados who would never have even dreamed of listening to a Queen record. However, as with *Live Killers*, Roger Taylor voiced his opinion, upsetting Freddie by dismissing the evening as 'terrible'.

At the party in the Crush Bar after the show, Freddie was introduced to one of the charity's patrons, Prince Andrew, and lost no time at all breaking the ice. The fun-loving royal was attempting to eat a dish of strawberries when Freddie screeched at the top of his voice, 'Phoebe, take it away!' 'Phoebe' was Peter Freestone, the ballet company's wardrobe assistant, whom Freddie would poach as his new *chevalier servant* before the evening was through. While they were chatting, the fringe of Freddie's scarf dropped into his drink. When Prince Andrew politely wrung it out, Freddie quipped, 'Thank goodness you've put me at my ease. Now I can use the odd bit of dirty language!' Then, when asked if he was going to sing one of the prince's favourite songs—he never got around to saying what this was—Freddie issued an ultimatum. He would sing, providing Andrew agreed to swing from one of the chandeliers, and later accompanied him and a few friends 'for a jar' at Heaven, the gay disco-club near Charing Cross.

The first request was denied, though Prince Andrew did agree to the club date. 'Mr Mercury's party were escorted to a private, very discreet table,' the then manager explained. 'They did not get up to dance, but drank, laughed and chatted until the early hours of the morning.'

At the end of November 1979, Queen embarked on what they

would call their 'Crazy Tour'—an alternative schedule of venues much smaller than the ones they had been playing in recent years, in order to establish a more intimate contact between themselves and their audiences. Unfortunately this caused monstrous problems with security, and with the police who each evening were faced with the possibility of a riot among fans who, unable to acquire tickets, turned up anyway hoping for a miracle with touts. There was even talk of some shows being cancelled altogether. The worst that happened, however, was a last-minute cancellation of the group's in-store signing at HMV's Oxford Street shop, on 12 December.

The tour opened in Dublin, where Freddie stole the show with a heart-rending arrangement of 'Danny Boy'—in contrast to his curtain-call, for which he was carried on stage on the shoulders of a minder dressed as Superman. It closed at the Alexandra Palace, three days before Christmas, with a noisy 'We Will Rock You', during which Freddie danced across the stage, pelting the audience with bananas, something he had seen his friend Divine do during a performance in New York. On Boxing Day, Queen played a charity gig at the Hammersmith Odeon—the first in a series employing different stars each evening, organized by Paul McCartney in aid of war-torn Kampuchea.

There was also a new regular man in Freddie's life. After Queen's 10 December concert at the Brighton Centre, Freddie, Paul Prenter and a few others had retreated to one of the resort's most popular gay spots, the Curtain Club. Here, he had ended up dancing cheek-to-cheek with a handsome, moustachioed 28-year-old courier named Tony Bastin. The pair spent that night in Freddie's hotel suite, and the singer is said to have fallen for him in a big way—certainly enough to warrant Bastin relocating to Freddie's flat, along with his beautiful ginger tom, Oscar, who some years later Freddie would claim as his own, long after he had stopped loving the man.

After the tour, Bastin formed part of Queen's entourage when they returned to Munich to resume work on their new studio album, *The Game*, and to work some more on the *Flash Gordon* soundtrack. *The Game*, of course, was an apt title for a group which seemed to be persistently in competition with itself, as Brian May later explained, 'We were always trying to take the next step—a million records this year, two million next. One night at Madison Square Garden this time, two next time. It's like being at school—get better marks and get a pat on the head. It was artificial, a game, a very comforting game.'

The guitarist also admitted that he and other members of the group often fought among themselves in the studio, adding, 'We'd hate each other for a while and get very angry with each other. I left the group a couple of times—just for the day, you know.' More serious were the rows about money, particularly over the dissention caused by Roger Taylor earning the same royalties for his composition on the B-side of 'Bohemian Rhapsody' as Freddie had earned for Queen's most celebrated song, though Freddie does not appear to have been too concerned about this, quipping, 'Four cocks fighting—how nice!'

At around this time, Freddie changed his 'tinsel and glitter' image, the subject of so much scorn from detractors. Throwing away his nail varnish and mascara, he cropped short his beautiful long hair and grew a bushy Burt-Reynold's-style moustache. 'It's a growth process,' he said, 'People grow up. After ten or twelve years you have to be seen to be growing up, and the people who've grown up with you can't suddenly say, "My God, he's still got long hair, and he's still wearing black fingernails and a lady's blouse!" I mean, it's ridiculous, and I would *feel* ridiculous.'

The 'new' Freddie made his début in the video for the single, 'Play Their Game'—Queen's first song to use synthesisers which was released in May. His change of appearance brought screams of disapproval from female and straight fans—particularly in the

United States, but sighs of ecstasy from gay ones—especially when Freddie began appearing 'topless', exposing an expanse of chest hair and flexing a more than generous set of muscles, a far cry from his 'Bo-Rap' days. Over the coming months, thousands of Freddie clones would begin flocking to discos across the world.

The Game, Queen's ninth album, was released at the end of June 1980, and went straight to the top of the charts—not that this prevented it from being attacked almost unanimously by the music press. Only *Sounds* seems to have truly recognized its worth, hailing it, 'A straight kick into the goal,,,,like winning the Men's Singles at Wimbledon.' The latter comment alluded to an idea floated by Queen the previous summer that they should give an out-of-season concert in the All England Club's revered Centre Court, a suggestion which was very quickly nipped in the bud by feisty club officials.

'Play The Game' attracted a great deal of heated criticism from a small section of overzealous fans who accused Queen of selling them short in breaking their promise, made back in 1973, that they would never use synthesisers. Effectively, these fans levelled, the group were heading in the same direction as their less-worthy contemporaries. All was well, however, when a group spokesman issued a statement to the effect that Queen were merely keeping abreast with modern technology—and in any case, their input of gadgetry was so minuscule that, rather than interfere with their instrument-playing, it only served to enhance it.

There were further, light-hearted protests a few days later when Queen embarked on a grueling, 46-date sell-out tour of North America. Still outraged by Freddie's new image, some fans pelted the stage with razors, packs of razor blades, and plastic bottles of nail varnish. The new look, however, opened new doors for Freddie's already considerable sexual appetite when the group arrived in Los Angeles for four shows at the Forum. Indeed, Paul Prenter later emphasized that Freddie had only changed his appearance in the first place in order to attract more of the butch-looking, well-built, hirsute men he had always preferred.

One of the first of this 'new breed' was John Murphy, a 30-year-old airline steward from Los Angeles whom Freddie had met during the flight from London to New York. Their affair would be brief, though long enough for Freddie's eyes to be opened one evening after Queen's concert, when Murphy and a group of leather enthusiasts took him on a foray into the seamier side of the city's gay scene. They took in such landmarks as the I-Beam, where most of the clientele wore skimpy, skin-tight vests—and the Black & Blue, where motorcycles were suspended from the rafters and many of the clientele turned up in full bondage-gear for the six-hour 'fuckathon', advertised in local contact magazines, and which began on the stroke of midnight when the doors of the establishment were closed to all but its regulars.

The Black & Blue, however, was pretty tame compared with The Glory Holes (aka South of Market Club), where Freddie met one of his idols, Rock Hudson, only recently out of the closet and desperately afraid of being recognised. Although Freddie and Rock were definitely not each other's types—the actor always had a penchant for muscular blonds, while Freddie almost without exception preferred what David Evans termed, 'Nice, well-built people with a good lot of meat on them'—this did not prevent them from engaging in a little harmless, mutual voyeurism.

Brought to the world's attention via the *Tales of the City* novels of Armistead Maupin, The Glory Holes consisted of several bars and any number of plywood booths, each with several holes, through which customers would insert their penises in anticipation of gratification from the other side. But if the recipient never knew who was 'pleasuring' him, the hundreds of men assembled on the balcony overlooking the booths were able to observe and applaud every movement. Both Freddie and Rock Hudson were offered membership of The Glory Holes but, much to the relief of their friends and entourages, both declined.

During this American tour, *The Game* became Queen's first Stateside Number One, and one of its tracks—John Deacon's 'Another One Bites The Dust'—shot to the top of the singles charts, where it remained for five weeks, selling three million copies and bringing their sales totals, to date, to thirty million singles and twice as many albums. In Britain the single reached Number 7, and like 'We Are The Champions' became a stadium anthem—aimed at the losing side, of course. The song also allowed Queen access to yet another musical style—funk—until then almost exclusive to black artists.

Hot on the heels of this success, 'Flash Gordon', taken from the soundtrack album released as a single in November 1980, made the Top Ten in Britain, but strangely made little impact on the American charts. Though by no means one of Queen's best songs, it was unusual in that it broke new ground as a novelty item, cleverly incorporating snatches of dialogue from the film, and lots of thunder-flashes—beside taking a risk by not featuring Freddie's voice on lead vocals.

Early in December, after a brief spell in Europe, Queen were the first act to play the recently-built 11,000-seater Birmingham New Exhibition Centre, where over two evenings the capacity crowd heard some of the *Flash Gordon* songs for the first time, synthesisers-et-al. To highlight the sci-fi element of their set, Freddie was carried on stage on the shoulders of his burly minder, who was dressed as Darth Vador. Because the group had not thought it necessary to seek permission to use the name and image of the *Star Wars* character as a publicity ploy the breach of copyright saw them served with a writ which, though irksome, evenually amounted to nothing.

The focal point of the evening, however, was Freddie's German leather shorts—some of his entourage had taken bets whether they would 'contain' him until the end of the show. They did, and afterwards he barked at an attendant reporter, 'Thank goodness I didn't get a hard-on, dear, otherwise I would have ended up singing like Yma Sumac!' This was also Freddie's British fans' first glimpse of his new image, of which James Johnson of the *Evening Standard* disapproved, writing, 'He *has* dropped some of his overtly camp affectations. But a new moustache suggests he is looking for a spare-time job as a waiter in the Fulham Road.'

This flying visit to Britain was tinged with tragedy when on 9 December—the day of the second of three concerts at Wembley Arena—Queen were informed that John Lennon had been shot dead outside his Manhattan apartment by a lunatic fan named Mark Chapman. The group at once elected to pay tribute to the man who, it was claimed, had been spurred into making a recent comeback only after listening to 'Crazy Little Thing Called Love'. With just hours to spare, Queen put together a special arrangement of Lennon's theme for peace, 'Imagine'. Such was the emotion that, halfway through, Brian May began playing the wrong chord and Freddie forgot the words. It was one of the rare occasions that he ever faltered on stage.

In February 1981, Queen played five sell-out shows at the Tokyo Budokan, and at the end of the month embarked on their biggest risk so far, a tour of South America. Barring several megatours by Latin stars Amália Rodrigues, Celia Cruz and Julio Iglesias, this part of the world had never hosted any mass concerts and indeed had no idea how to organize such a technical extravaganza—the lighting-rig alone of which demanded 300,000 watts of power—let alone supply a suitably sized venue.

Dubbed the 'Gluttons For Punishment' tour, the event required three months of forward planning, and an estimated budget of £750,000, added to which were the group's collective expenses of £25,000 a *day* once they hit the road. On top of this was the cost of supplying several tons of Astroturf to cover the 'hallowed' pitch of Buenos Aires' Velez Sarsfield soccer stadium, and of redesigning the tour logo—a pair of naked ladies, one of which was holding a banana suggestively—on account of South America's stringent anti-pornography laws, which were so strict that when a group of male fans opted to impersonate Freddie by strolling quite innocuously through the streets wearing shorts which by his standards would not even have been regarded as skimpy, they were promptly arrested, charged with gross public indecency, and jailed for two days.

Queen's arrival at Buenos Aires airport on 23 February was tantamount to them having been awarded freedom of the city—hardly surprising, perhaps, owing to the fact that every one of their albums was in the Argentinian Top Ten. For thirty minutes, flights were delayed as the intercom system broadcast Queen songs, and they were officially welcomed into a politically unsound Argentina by a presidential aide. Because of a strong terrorist element which had threatened to infiltrate the group's Spanish-Portuguese entourage, this official presence was a warning to would-be insurrectionists who had earlier protested about the 'capitalism' of a rock concert in a country which was rife with poverty. Subsequently, they were accompanied virtually everywhere by a squad of machine-gun toting military police. Freddie made light of this, posing for photographs with these hunky chaps and enthusing, 'All that meat and leather. Why don't you come to dinner tonight, dears?' He was perhaps surprised when several of them accepted the invitation—even more so at the end of the evening when, after toasting him with champagne, they tore of their official insignia and presented it to the group.

Queen's Buenos Aires concert on 28 February was filmed and broadcast the next morning to 40 million viewers throughout Argentina and Brazil. It ended with the British and Argentinian flags being unfurled at opposite ends of the stadium. Afterwards, the group attended a party hosted by the country's football manager, where they met one of their biggest fans, Diego Maradona, who posed for photographs with the group in the Union Jack T-shirt which Freddie had given him. Freddie's shirt, as he playfully pointed out to everyone, bore the 'Le Coq' logo.

The next day, the group were invited to an audience with President Viola, which brought the speedy response from Freddie, "How nice for them to have named a president after a pansy!' He was, however, said to have been angry at Roger Taylor's abrupt refusal on their behalf of Viola's obviously put-on generosity: 'We came over here to sing to the people, not to meet politicians.'

Following concerts at huge stadia in Mar del Plata and Rosario, and a return to the Velez Stadium which saw them all but beatified, Queen moved on to Brazil, where their promoter lost the battle to get them permission to perform at the Maracona Stadium in Rio de Janeiro, owing to a recent law forbidding the country's stadia from being used for anything other than sporting and religious events. Even the offer of a phenomenally huge donation towards the Governor of Rio's favourite charity failed to cut any ice. Therefore the group had to content themselves with a little sightseeing—and for Freddie, discreet visits to the city's gay village—until 20/21 March, when they reluctantly staged two concerts at the Morumbi Stadium, in Sao Paulo, each evening to a world-record crowd of 130,000, few of whom understood a word of English, yet who were still capable of belting out every word of 'Love Of My Life'.

To avoid the Brazilians' ruling that PA systems be stripped down, and searched for contraband—a time-consuming operation which resulted in a great deal of equipment being left in the country (which the wily Brazilians promptly rented out again)—immediately after their second show, while it was still dark and the South American promoter was busy filching the artificial turf from the stadium, Queen's one hundred tons of equipment was secreted into a juggernaut, then smuggled on to a private cargo-plane and flown out of the country.

Queen spent much of the summer in Munich, working on their next album, *Hot Space*, and generally living life to the full in their favourite location, enjoying a seemingly endless succession of all-night raves which saw them more often than not staggering into the studio bleary-eyed, but nevertheless producing their best work for some time. Roger Taylor followed the same theme too by releasing his début solo album, *Fun In Space*, which reached the Top Twenty, though the singles from it flopped. 'He *can* write songs,' observed *Sounds*, some time later when Taylor was still churning out chart failures, 'But he can't sing them like Freddie, which is why *Queen* gets the hits.'

Much more fruitful was Queen's project with David Bowie, who lived in Montreux near the Mountain Studios. Bowie had dropped in on one of their rehearsal sessions a while before, resulting in an impromptu jam-session which had produced at least one song, 'People In The Streets', though recording with Bowie, according to Brian May, was much less pleasurable. He told an American press-conference a few years later, 'David was aloof in the studio. He's a perfectionist. Working with him was a very difficult experience.'

Changed to 'Under Pressure', this very un-Queenlike duet would be released as a single at the end of October 1981, and not surprisingly go straight to Number One. Because Bowie and Queen were working in different parts of the world, however, and were unable to get together for a video, David Mallett was instructed to let his imagination run wild. This he did, compiling a 'stress' tapestry of mostly vintage film footage: tube station chaos, Nosferatu the vampire, collapsing tower blocks, the Wall Street Crash, poverty, soup kitchens and mass unemployment, assuaged by Hollywood on-screen kisses between Greta Garbo and John Gilbert, and Rudolph Valentino in *The Sheik*. The video was banned by the BBC, however, because it contained footage of IRA bombings in Belfast.

On 5 September, Freddie celebrated his 35th birthday in a huge suite in New York's plush Berkshire Hotel. Determined this time to be more flamboyant and outrageous than ever, he flew a hundred of his closest friends in from London—on Concorde, at £3,000 a throw—telling them, 'Don't worry about the cost, dears. The only thing you'll have to pay for will be the condoms!' Other friends were invited from his favourite gay clubs, including the a few 'turns' from the notorious Mineshaft, an establishment catering for enthusiasts of sado-masochism—which Freddie had recently designated his 'most cherished den of iniquity' since The Glory Holes, along with many New York and San Francisco saunas and bath-houses had been forcibly closed because of what was described by one tabloid as 'A mysterious, influenza-type malady which for some inexplicable reason is picking off only members of the gay community.' Freddie called his friends from the Mineshaft his 'New York gals', and thanked each of them for attending his party by rewarding them with a solid gold Cartier wristwatch.

On 25 September, Queen performed at the Poliedro de Caracas, in Venezuela, the opening date in the second leg of the South American tour. Here, political unrest was particularly acute. The former president, Romulo Ethancourt—hailed as 'The Father of Democracy'—was critically ill, and rumours that a revolution would erupt were he not to survive were rife. Three days later, Ethancourt died, plunging the country into a week-long period of mourning, during which virtually everything shut down, preventing Queen and their crew from leaving the country. There were further problems when the crew attempted to cross the border into Mexico. Due to restrictions imposed on the issue of visas, they were held up for several days—until the border guards were bribed into letting them through. If this was not enough, one week later –after Queen's triumphant show in Monterrey—the local promoter, José Rota, was arrested and sent to jail and the group compelled to put up the $25,000 to get him released –something they would not have done had they been able to see into the very near future.

Prior to Queen's two concerts in Puebla, their fans were rough-handled by security, who relieved them of any alcohol they were trying to smuggle in, then removed the films from their cameras and the batteries from their tape-recorders—only to pass this 'contraband' to the merchandise stalls within the stadium, which sold everything back to them at three times its original cost. The last straw came when José Rota informed the group that their fee for the second Puebla show was to be confiscated for tax reasons. Instead of moving to Guadalajara for their next concert, Queen flew to New York, leaving Rota and thousands of fans in the lurch, and swearing that they would never set foot in Mexico again.

At the end of November, Queen were invited to play two concerts at the 18,000-seater Montreal Forum. These were filmed, with the intention of turning the footage into a full-length feature film to be premiered in cinemas throughout North America during the summer of 1982, then put on general release in Britain and most of Europe. The project—directed by Saul Swimmer, the man responsible for the Beatles' *Let It Be*—was plagued with problems, mainly financial, from its conception. Fortunately for Queen's fans, but more especially for their detractors, this badly edited, poorly synchronised mish-mash did not see the light of day until 1884 when it was released as a video

—*We Will Rock You*. In November 1981, however, Queen were riding majestically on their highest wave. The single with Bowie was at Number One, as was their first compilation album, *Greatest Hits* and its accompanying video, *Greatest Flix*—not just in Britain, but throughout most of the world.

It was, however, the little things that touched Freddie's heart—the fact that Queen were so big that when an American fan sent a letter addressed simply to 'Queen, England'—it ended up at Buckingham Palace, whereupon the real Queen's comptroller forwarded it to them with the apology, 'Opened in error.'

'All I have to do is throw my carcass around the stage.'
(Redferns)

Six: Breaking Free

Queen's music was officially blessed by the classical world on 8 December 1981, when the Royal Philharmonic Orchestra & Choir played a concert of their songs at London's Royal Albert Hall. All the proceeds, including royalties from the subsequent album and video sales, were donated to leukemia research.

The group themselves spent much of the early part of 1982 in Munich, adding the finishing touches to *Hot Space*. In April they released a new single, 'Body Language' c/w 'Life Is Real', their belated studio tribute to John Lennon. From the fans' point of view—many of whom had given John Deacon's new funky sound a very definite thumbs down—the single and the subsequent album were the worst of Queen's reign and almost cost them their crown, reaching only Number 25 and Number 4 in their respective charts. The single fared better in America because of its promotional video featuring naked bodies smeared in baby oil, which sparked off a controversy when parents of younger fans denounced it as 'lewd' and petitioned the record company to change it. In South Africa it was denounced as 'immoral' and banned completely.

Freddie was always the first to admit a preference for one-night stands, or even flings lasting just a few hours, despite his regrets later in life that there had been but a handful of lovers who had been special. According to some reports he was always the nicest of men when crossed—but that his tantrums were often more to do with people being rude or taking advantage of him than in his actually being difficult. A few days after his death, an EMI spokesman spoke of the incident in the back of Freddie's limousine which occurred on the outskirts of Munich, during the late Spring of 1982:

We were trying to snort coke and watch the television at the same time. Then, Freddie's man switched channels, and he went bonkers, shouting and screaming. He told the driver to stop the car, then physically kicked the guy out into the road, leaving him stranded miles from anywhere. Then we went and found Freddie a new friend.

The new man, who replaced Tony Bastin as Freddie's regular lover, was a dark-haired, moustachioed young restaurateur named Winnie Kirkenberger, who actually dated him for several days before realizing who he was. And even after that, they refused to succumb to the privileged treatment which went hand-in-glove with being *chevalier servant* to one of the world's biggest rock stars, though he did accept a 'little gift'—a brand new Mercedes 560.

Freddie and Kirkenberger would remain lovers throughout most of the singer's sojourn in Munich, though they were never faithful to each other. Over the next three years there would be many three, and even four-in-a-bed scenarios, frequently drugs-and-drink-enhanced. At this time Freddie is said to have been spending upwards of £1,000 a week on vodka and cocaine just for his personal use. Paul Prenter spoke of an amusing occasion when, *en route* from New York to London on Concorde, Freddie discovered half a gram of cocaine in his shoulder-bag and, rather than be caught with it by customs officials at Heathrow, he decided to snort it there and then in his seat. 'After that, Freddie could have flown home by himself,' Prenter mused.

A row erupted in June, as Queen came towards the end of a European tour and the Falklands War reached its zenith. 'Under Pressure' was Number One in Argentina, and radio stations worldwide were playing one of their latest songs—'Las Palabras

De Amor', recorded as a tribute to their South American fans. The fact that some of lyrics were in Spanish was regarded as insensitive by opponents of the Argentinian dictator, President Galtieri, while the mere title of the duet with Bowie was declared 'propagandist' by him. Galtieri subsequently issued a decree banning all Queen records from the airwaves—but allowing them to be sold in the shops because the shops needed the revenue. The group were then informed that they would never be allowed in Argentina again. This upset Freddie deeply. Several of his Argentine one-night stands had since been recruited into military service and, completely a-political and regardless of the fact that he would probably never see them again, he was still concerned for their well-being. He told the press, 'This silly conflict is all about our young men killing *their* young men. Where's the *glory* in being blown to bits?'

In 1982 there would be just four British concerts, Queen's first in eighteen months: two in Edinburgh, one at Leeds' Elland Road football stadium, and one at the recently constructed Milton Keynes Bowl. Two others were cancelled: one at the Arsenal stadium because it was unable to obtain a live events licence, and the one at Old Trafford because of a shortage of portable toilets, these had all been commandeered by arguably Britain's most important tourist that year—the Pope.

The Milton Keynes show on 5 June was filmed by Tyne Tees Television. Broadcast on the first edition of Channel 4's *The Tube* on 7 January 1983, it provided an anodyne to the disappointing *We Will Rock You* video. Freddie, in fine vocal fettle and ruder than usual—at one stage of the concert he preferred his posterior to the audience, and several times 'masturbated' his microphone stand—belied the fact that he was still suffering from the shakes after a hair-raising flight to the venue, his first in a helicopter. Time and time again he leapt on to the scaffolding, balancing precariously high over the heads of the audience.

After this show, Queen paid £100,000 to hire London's Embassy Club for a 'shorts-and-suspenders' party. One of the guests was Diana Ross, whom Freddie had worshipped since her days with the Supremes. He was in such a hurry to get to the bash that, mindless of his terror, he agreed to another helicopter trip. There was, however, a last minute hitch: he arrived late, after an impatient Ross had already left.

From mid-July until September, Queen toured America and Canada. A notable event occurred on 23 July when the Mayor of Boston awarded them the keys to the city. On 25 September the group made their first and only appearance on television's *Saturday Night Live*, when Freddie accompanied himself on the guitar and offered a more than passable imitation of Elvis Presley with a rollicking 'Crazy Little Thing Called Love'. In October, the group paid another visit to Japan. Their final show there, at the Seibu Lions Stadium in Tokyo, was filmed and fourteen songs released on a commercial, Japanese-system-only video. All in all it was a busy year with seventy, costly extravaganzas in twelve countries—effectively their heaviest schedule in five years. But if fans were expecting more of the same over the next twelve months, they were in for a disappointment: at the end of 1982 the group announced that they would be taking six months off, maybe even a year. A combination of fatigue, the relative failure (compared with their other albums) of *Hot Space*, but above all artistic temperament had begun taking its toll.

For the music press, who had been sounding the death-knell for as long as anyone cared to remember, the fact that Queen might really have come to the end of the road was manna from heaven. Freddie, understandably, was on the defensive. Admitting that all their clashes centred around their oversized egos, and the fact that each member of the group more often than not wrote his contribution to a song while apart from the others, he told *Rockline*:

Sometimes I'll take one of my songs to Brian and he may put guitars on my song the way he wants to, not my way. So we'll fight. Sometimes we're the bitchiest band in the world! There's a lot of bad vibes, but in the end it always comes together. We have to fight, otherwise it would be a bit boring!

And on the matter of Queen's alleged split, he explained to the *Baghdad Observer*:

Some of us enjoy making solo albums, but we love getting together as a band and there is the obvious question: why kill the goose that lays the goose's golden eggs? Okay, so we won't be running around the stage when we're forty-five. That would be silly. But, if we do split up—well, dear, I suppose I'll just have to go off and become a striptease artist!

For the first seven months of the year, the four members of the group were content to go their separate ways. John Deacon devoted himself to his growing family: he and his wife Veronica already had three children, and would eventually have three more. Roger put much of his energy into racing boats and cars. In July he and his friend, Status Quo's Rick Parfitt, went to Monaco for the Grand Prix—but missed the race having spent the night in jail after being arrested for being drunk and disorderly. Brian joined up with a group of young musicians and released a mini-album, *Star Fleet Project*. Freddie lived life to the full in New York, where he now had a spacious, 43rd-floor apartment overlooking Central Park. 'New York is a Sin City,' he told the press, 'When I'm here, I can slut myself!' He did spend a little time, however, working on two songs with Michael Jackson at his home studios—in the days before eccentricity set in, the pair even went clubbing together. The idea was that the songs should appear on Jackson's *Thriller* album, or on Queen's next album, but the project amounted to nothing and the tapes, half-completed, still lie in a Hollywood vault.

In the summer of 1983, a six-date tour of South America was booked, unwisely in the aftermath of the Falklands War. Following heated exchanges over finances and politics, this was quickly aborted. By the middle of August –refreshed after their time apart and brimming with new ideas—Queen were working at the Record Plant Studios in Los Angeles on the score for the film, *The Hotel New Hampshire*, based on the novel by John Irving. This was to be directed by Tony Richardson, best known for *Saturday Night & Sunday Morning* and *A Taste Of Honey*. Married at the time to Vanessa Redgrave, Richardson—who tragically succumbed to AIDS just before Freddie—certainly showed more than a passing interest in Queen's frontman, but one which may not have been reciprocated, and which may have had something to do with the group's music not being used for the score, though much of it was put to better use when they incorporated it into their new album, *The Works*, which became the focal project of their ten-week stay at the Record Plant Studios. Released in February 1984, Queen's thirteenth album reached Number 2 in the charts. One song, Freddie's portentous, autobiographical 'Keep Passing The Open Windows'—a phrase used repeatedly by John Irving in his book—and sadly not as well-known as the other tracks on this album, was retained in its entirety.

At around this time, too, Queen changed their American record label. For some time they had been dissatisfied the way Elektra had been handling their output, so they signed with Capitol. Through Jim Beach, they forked out $1 million for the privilege of terminating their contract—a worthwhile sacrifice, they hoped.

Back in September 1983, one of the guests at Freddie's birthday party in Los Angeles had been the film producer, Giorgio Moroder, probably best known at the time for *Flashdance*. Moroder had recently purchased the rights to Fritz Lang's 1926 silent epic, *Metropolis*, with a view to restoring and re-releasing it the following year. The talents of Bonnie Tyler and several minor acts had already been commissioned. What Moroder now needed was some appropriate sci-fi music to augment the score and, having marvelled at their work for *Flash Gordon*, he approached Queen. The group made Moroder an offer he could hardly refuse: in exchange for exclusive rights to fragments of footage from the film, to do with as they wished, Queen would supply him with his music.

Metropolis, German-born Lang's prophesy of the Hitlerian regime, was a nightmare fantasy of machines, power and drudgery, inspired by the director's first impression of New York. Rulers and potentates live in skyscrapers, whereas the dehumanized workers toil underground, never resting in this symbolically controlled city. Anarchy erupts when Freder, the son of a leading industrialist (played by Gustav Frohlich, who bore an uncanny resemblance to Freddie) falls in love with Maria, one of the workers, resulting in the creation of a robotized Maria who incites her fellows to revolt—an insurrection which goes wrong when Freder supports them and not his father. Thus the city is left in ruins, and the industrialist is compelled to call a truce and swear a dramatic oath of friendship.

Several clips from *Metropolis* were incorporated into the video for the first single to be taken from *The Works*. Roger Taylor's song had started out as 'Radio Ka Ka', a title suggested by his small son who, upon listening to something on the radio that he had disliked, had applied the term he usually used when he wanted to go to the toilet. On Freddie's insistence, this was changed to 'Radio Ga Ga', though the theory behind Taylor's very absurd lyrics and engaging melody remained unchanged, as Freddie explained, 'It now seems that videos are more important than radio. But if videos *are* taking over, what is radio going to do? It's the downside of MTV. Every time you hear a song, you automatically picture the video. Of course, the funny thing about "Radio Ga Ga" is that we then had to rush out and *do* a video!'

The single was released at the end of January 1984, and peaked at Number 2 in the charts—robbed of the top spot by Frankie Goes To Hollywood's definitive gay-sex classic, 'Relax'. David Mallett's video, which cost whopping £110,000 to make, was filmed at Shepperton Studios. Fritz Lang had engaged a cast of 30,000 for his film, but Queen made to with a mere 500 extras—fans who were drafted in, dressed in white boiler-suits, sprayed with silver paint, and instructed to bow their heads in submission while clapping their hands repeatedly in unison with the group, a task which took twelve hours to complete because *Queen* kept getting it wrong. The four members were then cleverly incorporated into the film's theme, sometimes into the actual sepia footage: riding on the overhead motorway and, in blackout vignette representing a future holocaust, coming to life in an audacious Queen-only video kaleidoscope when a gas-masked family reach for their *Favourite Years* book. Freddie also took advantage of his resemblance to Gustav Frohlich by replacing him in the 'Hands Of Time" sequence, though by far the most ingenious piece of splicing comes when his face materializes within that of the robot, instead of Maria's. It is safe to say that, of all the Queen videos thus far—extant of 'Bohemian Rhapsody'—the one for 'Radio Ga Ga' was easily the most distinguished.

Hot on the heels of 'Radio Ga Ga' was the single, 'I Want To Break Free', and if David Mallett's video for this was only marginally less exciting than his last, it was more expensive to make and certainly proved controversial—though one is hard put

111

to imagine why. Its theme centred around the drudgery of a provincial Northern town, and was based upon Britain's longest-running soap-opera, *Coronation Street*.

Dreary back-to-back terraced houses and an exploding teasmaid open the scenario which features all four members of Queen in drag: Brian May, as Mother, in pink nightdress and hair-curlers; John Deacon, the Grannie who preoccupies herself with the newspaper headline, 'Rock 'n' Roll Earl Weds The Typist'; Roger Taylor, so utterly convincing and gorgeous as the bimbette schoolgirl that many fans refused to believe that it was him; and Freddie, the most outrageous of all—still moustachioed, wearing a skin-tight pink top covering his huge 'boobs', black leather mini-skirt, suspenders and high heels, vacuuming the carpet and prancing up and down with a feather duster until, flinging open the larder door, he enters a *Stars In Their Eyes* talent contest setting into the world of his dreams. Four-hundred miners in black boiler-suits and helmets (Queen fans, once more) escort him underground to the fawn's lair, where he recreates the Nijinsky role for the first time on celluloid—choreographed by Wayne Eagling and with a full *corps de ballet*—posturing, preening and body-swimming across a row of prostrated dancers, until the bubble bursts and he is transported back to working-class reality.

The music press, who over the years had gained a monopoly on mockery and frequently just being downright rude, purposely refused to see the funny side of Queen's *Carry On*-style humour. One publication branded them a 'bunch of transvestites', another accused them of inciting fans 'toward their own brand of blatant homosexuality', which was of course nothing less than cheap tabloid homophobia. 'I Want To Break Free' was also an exercise in record company greed, at a time when such practices were not as commonplace as they are today. Six different covers went on sale: four 7-inch singles depicting the individual members of the group, and two 12-inch singles with collective shots. Even so, it reached Number 3 in Britain, and was a phenomenal success around the world –particularly in South Africa, where in some countries (who as yet had not seen the video) it was adopted as an anthem against political oppression.

In the Spring of 1984, Freddie returned to Munich, where he set up court at the Arabella-Haus Hotel, flitting back and forth to the studio to work on his first solo album, a project with which he had been preoccupied for some time. In April, he appeared as part of a photo-feature for *Vogue*—about diamonds. A few weeks later he and Queen performed at the Golden Rose Festival, in Switzerland—an event which he loathed because all the artists were expected to mime to their records, and one which he turned into a farce by deliberately miming out of synch. And of course, Freddie's evenings were never short of riotous, almost exclusively turned over to hedonistic pursuit with Winnie Kirkenberger and Barbara Valentin—until the night of 22 May when, very much the worse for wear and wholly out of character, he got himself involved in a brawl and tore the ligaments of his leg, resulting in his having to spend three weeks in a toe-to-thigh plaster cast, incapacitated maybe, but still raising merry hell.

Only days after the cast was removed, Queen filmed the video for their next single, 'It's A Hard Life'. This opened with Freddie belting out a few bars from Leoncavallo's *I Pagliacci*, so naturally the setting was a masquerade ball—and while the other members of the group looked more distinguished than ever before in their brocades and ruffs, Freddie quite effortlessly managed to make himself the star of the show. An admirer of the legendary French revue star Mistinguett—famed for her fabulous legs, temper tantrums, and staircase tableaux at the Casino de Paris—he decided that he would emulate her, and commissioned a stunning one-piece scarlet outfit, cut to display one half of his torso and leaving one foot unshod, and decorated with twenty-six

113

large eyes, feathers, and a number of costly rare egrets which Mistinguett herself had worn in her 1938 revue, *Féerie de Paris*.

The single reached Number 6 in the charts, and was followed on 10 September by yet another track from the album, 'Hammer To Fall'—by the end of the year, every song on the album would have been put out as an A or B-side of a single, infuriating the critics and many fans, who bought them again all the same. On the same day the *We Will Rock You* video was released, along with Freddie's first solo single, 'Love Kills', from the Metropolis soundtrack. Though not as definitive as his later solo efforts, it was nevertheless a well-received début which soared into the Top Ten—something none of the other Queen members had achieved in their individual projects, which must have been very disconcerting for them at the time.

Queen's European tour, their first in over two years, opened at the Foret Nationale de Bruxelles on 24 August 1984 before progressing triumphantly through Eire, England, France, Italy (their first major concerts here) and Germany, until another "unlucky" 22nd—of September—when Freddie took an onstage tumble at Hanover's Europhalle, injuring the ligaments in his knee and forcing him to complete his set seated at the piano. He was treated at a local hospital, and advised to take at least a week's rest. Two days later, however, he was wowing fans in Berlin, and the tour continued without further hitch, closing in Vienna on the last day of the month. Queen then embarked on what would remain their most controversial project: twelve scheduled concerts in South Africa, at the Superbowl in Bophuthatswana's Sun City Complex.

The group's headstrong decision to work in a country torn apart by apartheid caused tremendous consternation among all sections of the media, as well as within the Musicians Union, who strongly advised them not to go. Sun City was a Las Vegas-style millionaires' paradise, part-financed by the country's government, situated smack in the middle of one of the most squallid, poverty-stricken townships in the world. Many great stars of the past had rallied to perform before mixed audiences—not just black entertainers such as Billie Holiday, Joséphine Baker and Lena Horne, but the likes of Marlene Dietrich, and Britain's George Formby, Dusty Springfield and Gracie Fields, but with them remuneration had always been secondary to fighting racial prejudice and segregation. Indeed, many of them had donated their fees to charity.

Effectively, *any* artist wishing to play Sun City was regarded as insensitive, oblivious towards the suffering of others and just downright greedy. What made this particular trip appear even more avaricious than it probably was were the varying statements given to the press before and after the event—Brian May declaring that Queen had always been completely nonpolitical, while John Deacon refuted this by saying, 'We're totally against apartheid and all it stands for.' Freddie only made matters worse by telling the press in what must have been the most foolhardy outburst of his entire career, 'There's *such* a lot of money to be made out there, dear!'

The first show took place amid great tension and stringent security on 5 October, though it was an unexpected disaster which almost brought the proceedings to a halt when, a few songs into their set, Freddie began experiencing pain in his throat. He struggled through till the end of the evening, but when the specialist flown in the next day ordered him to rest his vocal cords completely, or risk never being able to sing again, he backed down and the next four concerts at the 7,000-seater Superbowl were cancelled. While the other members of the group explored the world of the average Black South African—having learned that the incarcerated Nelson Mandela's African Nationalist Party had unofficially adopted 'I Want To Break Free' as its anthem—Freddie submitted to the peaceful atmosphere but

115

questionable pleasures of his hotel suite. There was one excursion, to the financially-strapped Kutlawamong School for Blind & Deaf Children where, completely unbeknown to his entourage, he handed over a huge sum of money—a cash donation which, along with the royalties from one of Queen's concerts, prevented the school from closure and made up for his earlier insensitive comment.

Upon their return to England, Queen were ostracised by the Musicians Union. Despite an impassioned speech from Brian May to their General Committee under the theme, 'Music should transcend *all* barriers, unfettered by race and politics,' Queen had to pay a hefty fine for breaking the anti-apartheid cultural boycott. Much worse than this, their names were added to the United Nations blacklist which ostensibly forbade them from ever setting foot in South Africa again while country was politically unsound. In this respect they were in good company: other names on the list included Dusty Springfield, who had angered the whites by performing the black soul she was renowned for—and George Formby, who had been so incensed by being ordered to stand at the side of the stage facing the white section of the audience, that he had cancelled the rest of his engagements and performed *only* to black audiences.

It was almost a case of 'out of the frying pan and into the fire' in January 1985, when Queen flew to Brazil to perform at the Rock In Rio Festival—a week-long extravaganza promoted as the biggest such event in rock history, featuring a large number of local groups, together with headliners such as Iron Maiden, Def Leppard and James Taylor. With crippling sincerity, Freddie told Sharon Feinstein of the *News of the World*:

> It was awe-inspiring and mind-boggling to be up there with all those people in the palm of your hand. But the other side of the coin is that, though I was surrounded by

masses of people who loved me, I must have been the loneliest person there. Can you imagine how terrible it is when you've got everything and you're still desperately lonely? That is awful beyond words.

Only recently, Queen had vowed never to visit South America again. This time, the deciding factor was not the fans or conquering new ground, but once again money, and lots of it. The group insisted on raking in even more by demanding the rights to their concert from the local television company who broadcast it live, so that they could release it on video. The first of their two shows took place on 12 January before a crowd of 250,000, at the Barra da Tijuca, in Rio—at two in the morning and in the pouring rain. This massive throng sang along and screamed for more all the way through their set until the curtain-call, 'I Want To Break Free'. Pandemonium ensued when, quite innocuously, Freddie minced on to the stage wearing the wig and the upper half of the costume he had worn in the video, which hardly anyone in this part of the world had seen.

First of all, a scuffle broke out when one of the security men started bullying a young man who emulated Freddie by shoving two oranges down his vest. Then, as if on cue, hundreds of fans standing near the stage began pelting the group with anything that came to hand—bottles, cans, stones and shoes—until Freddie saw the light and removed his 'falsies', whereupon they just as quickly settled down. He was later told the reason for their outrage: by performing *his* song in this way, he had offered the supreme insult against *their* anthem against dictatorship.

Unusually, too, the post-gig party—at the Copacabana Beach Hotel—was televised live, which may explain the reason why it was pretty tame by Queen's standards. One or two outbreaks of typical behaviour were captured on film, however, including Freddie's bitchy argument with Rod Stewart, who had apparently

117

gatecrashed the party, very quickly become drunk, then refused the summons to Freddie's table.

After Rio, Freddie spent several weeks commuting between London—clubbing and having riotous fun—and Munich, where he completed his first solo album, which he had decided to call *Mr Bad Guy*. The first single from this, 'I Was Born To Love You' c/w 'Stop All The Fighting', was released on 8 April, on the eve of Queen's tour of Australasia and Japan, and reached Number 11 in the charts. The video, again by David Mallett, featured hundreds of goose-stepping women wearing red plastic breastplates and high heels, and is said to have been inspired by the busty Barbara Valentin.

Queen's stay in Melbourne, between 16 and 20 April, almost ended in disaster when Freddie was asked to appear on *Countdown*, a popular television chat-show hosted by Ian 'Molly' Meldrum. The previous September, when his friend Divine had been about to tour Australia for the first time, Meldrum had called for a ban on the star—not because of his outrageous stage show, but because Meldrum had deemed Divine's films with John Waters, which he had never seen, as pornographic. 'Divi was convicted without so much as a trial,' Freddie had blazed at the time. 'Meldrum is a homophobe, and if ever *I* get the chance to meet him, I'll give him a piece of my mind!'

This never happened, though Freddie certainly embarrassed his host in front of millions of viewers when Meldrum asked him how he had persuaded the other members of Queen to drag up for the video of 'I Want To Break Free', responding, 'They ran for *their* frocks quicker than anything, dear!' The next morning, in some of the tabloids, the group were once more wrongly accused of 'perverting' fans.

By this time there was another regular man in Freddie's life. Jim Hutton was a 35-year-old hard-drinking Irishman who worked as a gentleman's barber at London's Savoy Hotel—a Burt

Reynolds clone of whom Freddie told a German reporter, 'Piaf did it, and so did Streisand. Now *I* have a hairdresser husband!'

Freddie and Hutton had met briefly at the end of 1983 in a Kensington gay club. According to Hutton, Freddie—whom he claimed not to have recognised, saying he had never even heard of Queen, which one finds hard to believe—offered to buy his near-lookalike a drink, only to be told, 'Fuck off!' The pair had since bumped into each other on numerous occasions, but the ice had not been broken until March 1985, when they had danced together at Heaven, one of Freddie's regular London haunts. Again according to Hutton, Freddie's chat-up line had been, 'How big is your dick?' Needless to say, they had spent the night together, though it would take a while for their relationship to become serious. Meanwhile, Hutton began spending his weekends with Freddie in Munich, where the singer was still seeing Winnie Kirkenberger—not out of mischief, it would appear, but because he did not have the heart to tell him that he had fallen in love with someone else.

Hutton does not appear to have minded being two-timed, but when Kirkenberger learned that there was another man in Freddie's life at least as cherished as he was, in a fit of pique he sold the car which Freddie had given him. For Freddie, this was the last straw. Soon afterwards he left Munich for good, and moved into Garden Lodge.

On 29 April 1985, *Mr Bad Guy* was released by CBS. The album was dedicated to Jerry, his recently deceased cat, and once he had acknowledged the other members of Queen 'for not interfering', Freddie insisted in adding to the sleeve notes, 'Special thanks to Mary Austin, Barbara Valentin for big tits, Winnie for board and lodging—Screw everybody else!' It reached Number 6 in the charts, surprising his critics from the music press who, unable to define a venture which was as far removed from Freddie's work with Queen as could be imagined, simply chose to defile it, and the unalterable fact that over the next six months, five of its tracks would be repeated on A or B-sides of singles, all comparative flops.

'Made In Heaven' (July) featured a David Mallett video wherein Freddie danced extracts from Dante's *Inferno*, and Stravinsky's *Le sacre du printemps*, in a specially built replica of London's Royal Opera House. 'Living On My Own' c/w 'My Love Is Dangerous' (September) had its video banned by CBS before any of Freddie's fans could see it and judge for themselves. It featured footage of his 39th birthday party at Henderson's nightclub in Munich, a Truman Capote-style Black-And-White Ball, but with the added dimension of cross-dressing. Freddie had forked out several thousand pounds to transform the club to his satisfaction—on top of the £50,000 bash itself. The furnishings were replaced, the toilets and dining-room completely renovated, and the place was decorated from top to bottom with black and white roses.

For the final single from the album, 'Love Me Like There's No Tomorrow' c/w 'Let's Turn It On', CBS attempted, but failed, to get the fans to part with their cash by giving away copies of the 12-inch version of the previous single with copies of the new one—just before EMI jumped on to the bandwagon by issuing *The Complete Works*, a limited edition boxed *intégrale* of twelve of Queen's albums. In the hope of ensuring sales, the bate this time was a complimentary album, *One Vision*, containing seven songs which had never appeared on albums—a privilege which set fans back a cool £70.

Many of Freddie's admirers, but not his close friends, had been surprised to learn from the album dedication that Mary Austin was still the most important person in his life, bearing in mind they were no longer lovers and that their split, according to the tabloids, had been acrimonious. Now, it emerged that he had recently changed his will, bequeathing her almost everything.

In a rare in-depth interview with Sharon Feinstein of the *News of the World*, Freddie poured out his feelings for this extraordinarily caring woman:

> We look at each other, and that's a wonderful form of love. I might have all the problems in the world, but I have Mary, and that gets me through. What better person to leave my fortune to when I go? Of course, my parents are in my will, and so are my cats, but the vast bulk of it will go to Mary. If I dropped dead tomorrow, Mary's the one person I know who could cope with my vast wealth. She's in charge of all my money and possessions, the chauffeurs, maids, gardeners, accountants and lawyers. All I have to do is throw my carcass around on stage.

'I am what I am, so is a stone. Them that don't like me can leave me alone.' (Redferns)

Seven: The Ultimate Driving Force

During the Spring of 1985, Jim Beach had been approached by former Boomtown Rats frontman-turned-do-gooder Bob Geldof, and asked if Queen might consider participating in his proposed summer extravaganza, *Live Aid*—all but finalized, with mass concerts at the JFK Stadium in Philadelphia and London's 72,000-capacity Wembley Stadium, to raise money for the starving millions of war-ravaged Ethiopia. 'Tell the old faggot it's going to be the biggest thing that ever whatsit happened,' Geldof told Jim Beach, with an irreverence which would continue over the next few months. This may have been why the group hedged, initially: there was no guarantee that the project would work, and Queen did not wish to become too involved in an enterprise which might make them appear foolish. It was only when Geldof spoke to them personally that they agreed to take part.

The event was finally fixed for 13 July, and each of the acts engaged allotted a 20-minute spot—a cue for a series of bitchy backstage cat-fights. Regardless of the fact that it was for charity, *Live Aid* proved an ideal vehicle for some faded stars, past their sell-by date, to resurrect their flagging careers. Morrissey, the frontman from the Smiths—who refused to augment the bill on principle—spoke up for the millions of British people who were against the event: 'If *Live Aid* had been organized to confront problems in *this* country, the event would not have taken place.' The DJ Jonathan King also came under attack for stating that Geldof had organized the whole affair as an exercise in self-glorification. Each of the acts, too, for purely selfish reasons, attempted to sweet-talk Harvey Godsmith, Geldof's promoter, into allowing them to close the show. Only Queen wanted to go on in the middle, a decision which earned them a great deal of respect from even their harshest detractors.

123

Whereas almost everyone involved with *Live Aid* threw their sets together will-nilly or plugged their latest records, Queen took the event seriously and hired the Shaw Theatre, near King's Cross, for three weeks of rehearsals, as intense and thorough as they would have been for any concert. Only a chance remark by Roger Taylor—'It'll make a pot of money for a wonderful cause, but make no mistake, we're doing it for our own glory as well!'—could have cast serious doubts on their benevolence. He was right, especially as *Queen Greatest Hits*, *The Works* and Freddie's *Mr Bad Guy* quickly returned to the charts after *Live Aid*—though he was of course only expressing aloud what most of the other acts may have been saying privately.

The dividend paid off handsomely, with no expense incurred on fancy lights and costumes. Freddie wore ordinary tight-fitting denims and a white athletic vest, and watched by a world-audience of two-billion, Queen stole the show, demoting everyone else on the bill to the status of also-ran. Elton John, David Bowie and Madonna, superstars in their own right, were dismissed by the *Independent* as 'buskers in makeshift combos'. In one fell swoop, Queen righted the wrongs perpetrated by their visit to South Africa, at least as far as the press were concerned. Bob Geldof told a press-conference, 'Queen were absolutely the best band of the day, whatever your personal preference. They had the best sound, they played best, and it was the perfect stage for Freddie. He could ponce about in front of the whole world.' What he did not add, a fact which was observed by almost every journalist who witnessed the event, was that Freddie Mercury was the heart and soul, the ultimate driving force behind Queen—that it had been *his* day, and his day alone.

Live Aid was the first rock concert that Jim Hutton had attended, and he reflected proudly, 'To see Freddie up there controlling that crowd, tears welled up and the hairs on my neck stood on end.' Immediately after the event, Queen were approached by Russell Mulcahy, then known only for his promotional pop videos, and asked to contribute to the soundtrack of his first feature film, already in production. Starring heart-throbs from different generations—Sean Connery and Christopher Lambert—*Highlander* was a swashbuckling fantasy recounting the bloodthirsty adventures of a time-travelling Scottish warrior and his fight for supremacy against other immortals.

As usual, the group demanded top-billing: they would provide a minimum two songs, but only if Mulcahy used one of them for the title-track. The director in fact compromised by having Queen do the entire soundtrack for the film and, as with *Flash Gordon*, they decided that all the songs would be slightly amended and released an album. *A Kind Of Magic* would fare even better than its soundtrack predecessor, topping the British charts during the summer of 1986 and reaching the Top Ten in some forty other countries. As for *Highlander*, it received a privileged world premiere—not in a huge cinema, attended by the glitterati of the entertainment word, but in Great Yarmouth at Queen's very first International Fan Club Convention.

The group's choice for their début single from the album, in retrospect, was not a wise one. Although 'One Vision' had as its basis Martin Luther King's famous 'I Have A Dream' speech, the media immediately drew parallels with *Live Aid*, and accused Queen of cashing in on a tragic situation—particularly as the idea for the 'One heart, one soul, just one solution' lyrics had come from Roger Taylor, so soon after his admission that one of the group's main reasons for appearing in *Live Aid* had been for personal glory.

Several publications insisted that all the royalties from 'One Vision' be donated to *Live Aid* because the song's press-release declared it had been inspired by the event. What they overlooked completely was the fact that one of their *Live Aid* songs, 'Is This The World We Created', had earned thousands of pounds for the Save The Children Fund. Two other Queen songs had been included on the album for Greenpeace, enabling their names to be engraved on a commemorative obelisk—in Antarctica. Neither did the media pay much attention to Freddie's contribution to *Fashion Aid*, which took place at the Royal Albert Hall on 5 November. Freddie wore a braided jacket made by David and Elizabeth Emmanuel, while his escort for the evening—actress Jane Seymour—wore a resplendent wedding dress not dissimilar to the one the couturiers had made for Princess Diana. Freddie was in his element, posing for photographs with Shirley Bassey and 'sharing a jar' with one of his idols, Julie Goodyear, aka *Coronation Street*'s brassy barmaid, Bet Lynch.

There were further problems at the end of the year when the artistic director of Bophuthatswana's Sun City Complex, Hazel Feldman, visited London with the intention of recruiting a number of artists, including Queen, for a return visit to South Africa. No one may now be sure if any discussions actually took place within the group, though Feldman did announce to the music press, 'A return appearance by Queen should not be ruled out.' In order to extricate themselves from what might have become an explosive political situation, the group were compelled to issue a formal statement, 'Queen categorically state that they have no plans at present to return to Sun City. They wish to make it plain that they have a total abhorrence of apartheid.' And this time there were no flippant comments from Freddie or Roger Taylor.

Much of Queen's time was currently being spent working on the new album, though all four members of the group were involved in solo projects. Freddie was commissioned to work on the score for a German film, *Zazou*—contributing a duet with an unknown singer named Jo Dare. He reacted to photographs and features appearing in the press concerning his 'new' escort, Barbara Valentin, telling one journalist, 'Barbara and I have formed a kind of bond which is far stronger than anything I've shared with a lover in the last six years.' Like most people, the reporter was not aware of the fact that the pair had been close for several years, or of Freddie's involvement with Jim Hutton, who had by now moved into Garden Lodge, where he would be cautiously introduced to non-friends as 'Mr Mercury's gardener'.

Several years after Freddie's death, Hutton would upset a lot of people by announcing, 'From then on, we lived together as man and wife for the rest of Freddie's life.' It would however prove a sometimes stormy six years, with more than a few tears and many arguments, most of them quite vociferous and, on at least one occasion, physically violent. 'Jim was a sweet guy, but he drank like a fish,' Jacky Gunn said, 'And when drunk, he was an ugly drunk.' Freddie's friend Jim Jenkins went further:

> Jim was particularly embarrassing at some of the Queen conventions. He would say all sorts of dirty things in front of little girls, about some of the things he and Freddie had supposedly got up to. Once, my friend Ian Bowman, one of the nicest people I've ever met, tweaked Jim's nipple just for fun. He started screaming, 'Only one person's ever been allowed to do that to me!' and there was almost a fight. He was very nasty.

At this time Freddie also loaned his considerable talents to his friend Billy Squier's *Enough Is Enough* album, vocalizing on 'Love Is The Hero' and collaborating on 'Lady With The Tenor Sax'. Much more interesting, however, were the two songs he recorded which had been written by a much closer pal, Dave Clark, the singing drummer from the Sixties pop group, the Dave

Clark Five. Clark—who once strangely hailed Freddie as 'The Piaf of the Eighties'—was working on a stage musical, *Time*, for Cliff Richard, but the songs on the soundtrack album were to be performed by independent artists. Besides cutting the title-song, Freddie donned the proverbial hair-shirt for 'In My Defence', a combination of an overpowering melody and a sadly restricted lyric which was nevertheless, in retrospect, a personal credo. 'In my defence, what is there to say?' he asks, before declaring, 'All the mistakes we've made must be faced today...'

The video for *Time* was filmed at the Dominion Theatre in London's Tottenham Court Road, where the show was playing to packed audiences every night, with Cliff Richard in the starring role and featuring a hologram of Sir Laurence Olivier. (Here, in May 2002, Ben Elton, Brian May and Roger Taylor's musical extravaganza, *Queen: We Will Rock You* opened to an almost universal panning by critics—yet it would break the theatre's box-office records.) One afternoon there was an incident when Freddie turned up at a matinée performance of *Time* with a friend. Remembering his visits to the local cinema during his teens, he decided that he wanted to be 'the girl with the tray' and, not content to do things by halves, borrowed a white smock from an usherette and purchased the entire contents of an ice-cream tray. He then paraded up and down the aisles of the theatre, doling out free tubs and cones. However, to expedite the job as soon as he was recognized, he suddenly started throwing them in all directions. Some members of the audience saw the funny side of this and began throwing them back. Others disapproved, sending the theatre manager their dry-cleaning bills. When Sir Laurence Olivier heard of Freddie's exploits, he and his actress wife John Plowright invited him to their home for dinner. Later, they recalled that it had been the most enthralling evening, with 'oodles of laughing, ribald jokes, and lots of healthy effing and blinding'.

128

Queen's next single from their forthcoming album was its title-track, Roger Taylor's 'A Kind Of Magic'. Released on 17 March 1986, it reached Number 3 in the charts. The video, directed by Russell Mulcahy, was his way of thanking the group for their splendid work on *Highlander*. Filmed at the then not in use Playhouse Theatre in London's Charing Cross, the video featured Freddie as a Bruantesque magician who, surrounded by the animated characters of the group from the album cover, transforms then from derelicts to musicians, then back again. The American sampler single, 'Princes Of The Universe', chosen by CBS against Queen's wishes, proved a flop despite an appealing video for which Christopher Lambert recreated his *Highlander* role. Even so, the group were truly in seventh heaven. *A Kind Of Magic*, their most innovative album in years, was released on 2 June, and regardless of the usual hammering from the music press went straight to the top of the British charts, quickly following suit in Australasia and throughout much of Europe, but barely scraping into the Top Fifty in the United States, one country which had always been full of surprises where record sales were concerned.

That year's 'Magic Tour', arranged and promoted by Harvey Goldsmith, was the biggest, best and costliest ever. The venues were vast, the concerts triumphs of mind over matter—not just for Queen but for the road crews and lighting technicians, who were responsible for hauling the 100-foot stage back and forth across Europe to a staggering twenty-one venues, and for erecting and maintaining an increasingly complicated two-ton lighting rig, an operation alone which took forty hours to complete.

The tour kicked off on 7 June at Stockholm's Rasunda Stadium—a shaky start marred by the heckling of hundreds of anti-apartheid demonstrators and, in the street outside the venue, a noisy protest march by what the press dubbed 'former admirers who have seen the light'. These tried to badger genuine fans into boycotting the show. Queen's set, too, was more varied than usual—not just a plug for the new album but including several old hits which had not been aired for years, along with a nifty rock 'n' roll medley. 'We're probably the best live band in the world, and we're going to prove it,' an ever-cocky Roger Taylor boasted to the press, adding to Freddie's earlier disclosure, 'We are the Cecil B DeMille of rock!' As for Freddie's curtain-calls during this tour, the term 'audacious' seemed grossly inadequate. Wearing what many fans believed was genuine royal apparel—an ermine-lined cloak, jewelled crown, and carrying an orb and sceptre, all designed by his friend Diana Mosely—Freddie was every inch the King of Queen!

The tour progressed through Holland, France, Belgium, Germany and Switzerland, with the elements clearly on Queen's side. Then on 5 July they played Slane Castle, on the outskirts of Dublin, where it stayed fine just long enough for Freddie to pose for photographs wearing his crown and, in some shots, looking decidedly un-regal with a cigarette dangling from the corner of his mouth. The rain that evening had an adverse effect on the crowd, who barely tolerated the support acts—including Chris Rea—before taking their frustration out of each other halfway through Queen's set. Four days later the group played one of the 'smaller' venues on their circuit—Newcastle's 40,000-seater St James Park, the entire proceeds of which they donated to Princess Anne's Save The Children Fund. Then, on 11-12 July they appeared before an audience of 144,000 at Wembley Stadium—this had sold out within hours, and was filmed and recorded in its entirety.

At Wembley, in spite of more rain—'I expect they paid the heavens handsomely for the special effects,' quipped one reviewer—the fans had the time of their lives, particularly when halfway through the show four massive helium-filled dummies of the group were launched from the stage. Three failed to get out of the stadium. Claimed by the crowd, they were burst, ripped to shreds and squabbled over as battle trophies. 'Freddie' turned up the next morning—in a back garden in Chelmsford.

No great Queen performance could be put to bed without the backstage party—an £80,000 bash at the sumptuous Roof Gardens, above the Marks and Spencer store in Kensington High Street, where no amount of opulence could prevent Freddie and his friends from having the most outrageous time of their lives until dawn, though for once he played things down by arriving with Mary Austin, much to Jim Hutton's dismay. From that day, according to several of Freddie's close friends, the man and woman in his life would never see eye to eye.

Queen's guests were escorted to the main party area by bellboys and busty women wearing nothing but body-paint designs executed by the artist Bernd Bauer, flown in from Munich for the occasion. Drag queens were everywhere, some so convincing that several straight men were given nasty shocks in the anteroom which had been set up for 'personal' services. Cocaine too was in ready supply—served on silver platters by naked dwarves. In the ladies' powder-room, the 'attendant' was a young man in chains and a studded leather posing-pouch, which Freddie had purchased from the Zipper store in Camden Town. Most outrageous of all, however, were the nude girls in cages in the club's gardens, and the topless blondes offering hand-relief in the gentleman's lavatories. Revellers Gary Glitter, Mel Smith, Griff Rhys-Jones and Limahl are said to have lapped up every precadillo thrown at them, though Cliff Richard is thought to have frowned on such behaviour. On the other hand, everyone adored the main event when, in a hilarious spoof, Queen took to the floor as 'Dicky Heart & The Pacemakers', aided by *Sun* Page Three girl Samantha Fox and Gary Glitter, for an impromptu rock 'n' roll jam.

After their concert at Manchester's Maine Road football stadium on 16 July, Queen played Cologne, then Vienna, where Freddie was joined by Mary Austin. From here they travelled—via the Danube, on Russian President Mikhail Gorbachev's personal hydrofoil—to their next venue, the 80,000-capacity Budapest Nepstadion, which had been built by Stalin.

Queen's Hungarian admirers were especially demanding. Whereas great stars such as Marlene Dietrich, Louis Armstrong and Charles Aznavour had taken drastic cuts in their fees here to enable fans to be able to afford to see them, Queen's phenomenal running costs and alleged unwillingness to submit to such a thing resulted in each ticket for their show costing the equivalent of four weeks' wages. None of their records had ever been released in Hungary: they were imported from Yugoslavia, which had already imported some of them from Britain and America, and prices were frequently exorbitant. 'They will *have* to be good, all things considering,' warned one newspaper.

Beginning with their official reception at the British Embassy, every step of Queen's visit was captured on celluloid and used to augment their *Live In Budapest* video, a concept which was considerably better filmed and edited than their earlier Rio video. The group were seen waving to their fans from their boat, signing the City Book, and sunbathing. John Deacon managed to chat with a shy little English girl, Roger Taylor participated in a go-kart race without a crash helmet, and Freddie and Mary Austin were filmed buying prints and antiques. Much of this footage was shot by the state-owned Mafilm Company, using every single television camera available in the country—besides being incorporated into the video, the footage was used for documentaries broadcast to Czechoslovakia, Romania and the Soviet Union. But if there was a general feeling of camaraderie among the local media, who could not have done enough to make the group's stay in Budapest a memorable one, the behaviour of the British press over which of their members should be afforded the most preferential treatment, was utterly deplorable. Worst of all were the 'lower denomination'—Freddie's term for the music press—though he had his revenge on these by having them issued with badges bearing the somewhat grandiose-sounding inscription, 'Brygada Bosmec', which they sported with pride until learning from the local police that *bosmec* was Hungarian for 'Fuck off.'

Queen's support act at the Nepstadion was their most unusual ever. Z'zi Labor was a local repertory group of forty female folksingers whose average age was fifty, and who performed in traditional costume. Freddie became pally with two of them, regardless of the language problem, and through an interpreter accepted a date. He learned the words to 'Tavaszi Szél Vizét Araszt', a popular ditty, and promised to add it to Queen's set, providing Z'zi Labor learned and performed the Rolling Stones' 'Honky Tonk Woman', which they did. The Hungarian song would be sung frequently throughout Queen's visit, though during the actual concert Freddie had to rely on reading the words off the palm of his hand. Though very brief, with a poignant accompaniment from Brian May this beautiful little piece brought the house down.

Although he joked that he had been unable to even go to the toilet without being trailed by the press, Freddie did manage to evade media attention while sampling the more personal delights of Budapest. There were only three know gay bars in the city in those days, all totally respectable, though on account of the country's homophobia they were accessible only through a discreet telephone call, followed by a password spoken into the back-door intercom. There was also a not so reputable underground bath-house, the setting a few years later for any number of gay porn films and which Freddie considered visiting, but at the last moment decided this might be going *too* far.

Queen's concert on 27 July was breathtaking, but restrained because Hungarian audiences were not allowed to respond as enthusiastically as Western ones. The police in charge of security carried sub-machine guns, and a large portion of the audience comprised the Young Guard, a youth organization not especially concerned with who was on stage, but with the fact that this was the very first rock concert to have been staged in the Eastern bloc. They had been particularly impressed by an earlier statement issued by Gheorghiu Lakos, the local promoter: 'This is the new urban folk music. There is no clash between rock and socialism here. It is the culture of workers and students, and will improve the image of our country.

On the positive side, closest to the stage were 800 genuine fans who had risked the journey into Budapest from two towns across the Ukrainian border, and it was they who whooped and cheered the most, though apparently not enough, according to *Time Out*'s John Gill, who observed, 'Even Freddie's posturing has lost any sense of camp and ribaldry. The mike-as-penis extension routine is as clean as *The Jimmy Saville Show*, and you could show the bump 'n' grind passages to your gran.'

After Budapest there should have been just four concerts left in Queen's schedule: one in Fréjus in the South of France, and others in Barcelona, Madrid and Marbella. Harvey Goldsmith, however, well aware that he was probably on to the biggest money-spinner of his career—thus far the tour had grossed in excess of £10 million—added a last-minute concert at Knebworth Park, a country house near Stevenage, for 9 August, which would give them their largest ever British audience. According to the police reports, which claimed that the event had been oversubscribed, 193,000 fans flocked to the grounds, creating one of the worst traffic-jams seen in Britain for years. For the fans, it was worth every hassle, and there was plenty to do before the group took to the stage as Goldsmith had provided beer-tents, a dance-hall, and even a funfair.

In fact, Queen stole the limelight without playing so much as a single note—while one of the warm-ups, Big Country, were halfway through their set, the group flew overhead in their custom-painted *Kind of Magic* helicopter, causing utter pandemonium. One young woman went into labour and had her baby in the field and, more seriously, another fan became involved in a brawl and was stabbed, bleeding to death before help arrived.

Knebworth Park proved an exhausting but inspired event for everyone on both sides of Queen's showbusiness fence, though the press were by now in agreement that, more than ever, Queen had become more or less a one-man outfit. Andy Stout wrote in *Sounds*:

> Queen are a seriously good live act. Freddie Mercury is perhaps one of the best singers and frontmen rock has ever had. The rest of the group may be musically great and groovy, but they're also sodding boring.

Before leaving the stage, Freddie had told the audience, 'Thank you, you beautiful people. Goodnight, sweet dreams. We love you!' In effect, he was sealing Queen's swansong as a live act, for what no one in that crowd knew was that they were seeing their beloved idols for the very last time.

Meanwhile, for the group the remaining months of 1986 passed quickly, though not uneventfully. Brian May and John Deacon, committed to respective solo projects, vied for tabloid headlines with exposés on their private lives—May becoming involved with *Eastenders* actress Anita Dobson, now that his marriage had collapsed, Deacon alleged to be recovering from a nervous breakdown brought on by overwork.

Freddie devoted much of his time to the ongoing renovations at Garden Lodge, taking an active interest in the landscaping of his garden and the construction of the large pond which would soon house his collection of Koi carp—taking a break only to organize his birthday party.

This particular birthday—Freddie's fortieth—was feted with a Mad Hat Party, and was tamer than most of the others. Now that he had revised his sexual proclivities there were no known illegal substances, no freak entertainers, no nudity and sex, just honest-to-goodness fun with 200 friends. Joe Fanelli, in charge of the catering, wore a creation decorated with dozens of Belgian chocolates, and Mary Austin turned up in a sword-pierced matador's hat. Most important of all was Jim Hutton's surprise—a plain gold wedding-band which Mary is said to have approved, but which for obvious reasons was never worn in public, though it does turn up in several private photographs.

After the party, Freddy and Hutton 'honeymooned' in Japan—a three-weeks, £1 million "shopathon" during which Freddie's purchases were so extensive that most of them had to be taken straight from the stores to a warehouse, where they were crated and shipped to England. And naturally, there were the obligatory trips to the Ginza, where Freddie visited several tea-houses and renewed his acquaintance with Miwa, at his famous club. As a belated birthday present, Miwa performed 'Non, je ne regrette rien' and 'Tu ne sais pas aimer' (You don't know how to love)—the latter a Damia *chanson* which, ironically, would be used in France as the theme-song for AIDS awareness.

The following afternoon, there was a subdued joint birthday party for Freddie and his Japanese hostess—personal assistant, Misa Watanabe—at her home. This pleased him no end, though Watanabe's surprise for that evening did not go down well at all: she had arranged for him to be guest of honour at the premiere of an all-Japanese production of Andrew Lloyd Webber's *Cats*, and to attend the backstage party, a hysterical affair which saw him mobbed by members of the cast. Freddie was further angered a few days later when visiting a museum in Chiba, famed for its collection of exquisite blue-and-white 'Hizen' porcelain plates. He tried his utmost to persuade the curator to sell him some of these, but to no avail. All he ended up was a copy of the catalogue, and a red face.

The couple's flight home to London, diverted to Alaska because of industrial action, the non to Munich on account of adverse weather conditions, was an arduous 24-hour ordeal, therefore neither man was prepared for the sudden rush of reporters which greeted them at Heathrow. Freddie had recently taken a HIV test (allegedly his first) and news of this had been leaked to the press. George Kozikowski, of Harley Street's Jean Shanks Clinic, had apparently disregarded the hippocratic oath by telling the *News of the World*, 'I didn't know he was here until his name unfortunately appeared on a form.

This resulted in the tabloid hacks sharpening their quills in preparation for what could turn out to be their second major "gay plague" attack on a well-loved personality. The previous October, Rock Hudson had died of AIDS, aged 59, opening the floodgates to arguably the most hateful, prejudiced and disgraceful newspaper headlines ever printed. The British media's reaction in particular towards his death could not have been more inhuman and undignified. 'He was one of the gentlest, kindest men in Hollywood, and all those journalists should burn in hell for the bile they printed about him when he died,' Marlene Dietrich told me.

The *News of the World* ran an exclusive: QUEEN STAR FREDDIE IN AIDS SHOCK, though the editorial added the test had proved negative, a pathetic consolation after the unforgivably misleading headline, and that Freddie and girlfriend Mary Austin were living as a couple at Garden Lodge. Feeling betrayed, Freddie reacted as expected, snarling at reporters brandishing copies of the *News of the World*, and at photographers who tried to snap him at close range for any tell-tale signs, 'Do I *look* like I'm dying of fucking AIDS? I haven't got any sexual disease. Leave me alone!' In truth, he looked remarkably well, despite the long flight, but his outburst, minus the expletive, appeared as a headline in the *Sun* on 14 November, together with his statement, 'I'm perfectly fit and healthy, thank you. I don't know what anybody has said, but it's all so silly. Of course I'm concerned about my health. Isn't everybody?'

Even so, such media speculation terrified Freddie, compelling him to tone down his lifestyle and be constantly on his guard. There would be fewer wild parties, no one-night stands, and many evenings spent at home in front of the television. 'I've stopped going out,' he said, 'I've almost become a nun. I was extremely promiscuous but I've stopped all that. What's more, I don't miss that kind of life.' David Evans, a frequent visitor to Garden Lodge said, 'Privately, Freddie would talk about anything but his work—his paintings, shows he had seen, places he'd been to, stars he'd met, how awful Sarah Ferguson looked in her wedding dress. All the camp things that gay boys talk about, but *never* his work.' Freddie's producer friend, Mike Moran, added:

> Freddie may have been a very famous guy, but he only had a small circle of friends, and he led a very private life. The same people were there all the time: Mary, my wife Linda and myself, Peter Straker and Dave Clark, Freddie's doctor Gordon Atkinson and his boyfriend, Jim and Claudia Beach. The others from the band didn't visit often, except Brian with Anita Dobson. Then occasionally there would be Tim Rice and Elaine Paige, or Barbara Valentin.

138

A few days after returning from Japan, Freddie received another shock when John Murphy arrived for a holiday in London. Although they were no longer amorously interested in each other, Freddie and he were still very good friends, and each time he visited Los Angeles Freddie would dine with Murphy and his partner, James Wynethorpe. Now, Murphy dropped the bombshell that they were both dying of AIDS. Worse was to come, for no sooner had Murphy settled in at Garden Lodge than he was summoned home—Wynethorpe's health had suddenly deteriorated.

In fact, it was John Murphy who died first, on 11 November 1986, followed a few weeks later by his lover. Freddie was devastated, yet no sooner had this dreadful news sunk in than he received a telephone call from Brighton. Tony Bastin had also succumbed to the disease. Freddie told the press:

> So many of my friends are dying of AIDS. Others won't last much longer, and I'm terrified that I'll be next. I know it's silly, but each time I make love I jump into the shower and scrub myself clean. Not that it's going to make any difference—I mean, if I've got it already, what can I do?

Despite these tragedies, work had to go on and the next few years would find Freddie at his peak, vocally and artistically. At the beginning of 1987 while *Live Magic*—an edited compilation of highlights from Queen's last tour—was riding high in the charts, Freddie began a hugely successful working partnership with Mike Moran, the producer of his *Time* songs, first at Moran's home studio, then at London's Townhouse Studios where he recorded Buck Ram's chart-topping 'The Great Pretender', which he had written for the Platters in 1955. Freddie was amused that the American group had recorded it on the Mercury label, but he is known to have preferred the cover-version by British singer Ann Shelton, who took it into the charts the following year. Released on 23 February, it is perhaps the best-loved and most widely known of all Freddie's solo songs, and peaked at Number 4 in the charts. The video was his most stylish since 'It's A Hard Life', and featured yet another staircase descent, together with 400 Freddie cut-outs, and cameo appearances by Roger Taylor and Peter Straker, wearing drag.

Coinciding with the release of 'The Great Pretender', Freddie granted an interview with one of the few journalists he trusted, David Wigg of the *Daily Express*, who over the past year or so had witnessed several of the singer's tantrums—one when, after his microphone had cut out in the middle of a song, Freddie had stormed into his dressing-room to hurl a steam-iron through a full-length mirror—another at Garden Lodge, when in a fit of pique he had thrown a valuable antique Japanese vase through the window before collapsing on his bed in a flood of tears. Now the conversation was quite perturbing. Not only had he lost John Murphy and Tony Bastin, another friend was dying of AIDS—Kenny Everett's lover Nicolai Grishanovitch, whom Freddie had nicknamed 'The Madam From Minsk', succumbed to the disease the following year. Admitting that he had just tested negative again for HIV, Freddie told Wigg:

> AIDS has changed my life. I'm not as promiscuous as I used to be. I've adopted an intelligent approach towards sex –after all, I've had lots of lovers, male and female, though all of them have gone wrong. I think anyone who has been promiscuous should have a test. You can still have fun—you can't expect people to just give up sex, but I think the message people are trying to get over, this thing about safe sex, is worthwhile.

But, had Freddie found that crock of gold at the rainbow's end, that special person to share the rest of his life with and, more importantly, if the right person came along, would he be willing to make the ultimate sacrifice? Some months before he had confessed that only two 'creatures' had ever returned the love he had given them: Mary Austin and Jerry, his cat. Now, he told David Wigg:

Money can't buy you love, and the more money one makes, the more miserable one becomes. Money attracts all kinds of wrong people. I would not sacrifice my career if a partner wanted me to. It's my career that keeps me going. What else would I do? Dig weeds, get fat and be beautifully in love? No, I'd like to remain as successful as I am, write beautiful songs and be in love—not that it's worked up till now, though I'll keep on trying. I've cried rivers, I may be hard on the exterior, but I'm very soft-centered. I'm also a very possessive person. I can go to great lengths, trying to be loyal just to prove a point, but the moment I find someone has betrayed me, I go the other way. Betrayed, I'm an ogre!

Title courtesy of the great French chanteuse, Barbara (1930-97)

Eight: Shake The Foundations From The Skies!

Freddie's next project astounded fans and friends and left critics wondering if he had finally gone mad. His almost manic passion for opera had begun in Panchgani when as a teenager he had stunned school chums by listening to the pre-war recordings of Clara Butt and *bel canto* coloraturas Amelita Galli-Curci and Elvira de Hidalgo. The latter had been instrumental in launching Maria Callas' career and, in July 1965, Freddie had been talked into seeing Callas' *Tosca* with Tito Gobbi at London's Covent Garden—a friend of his father's had bought two tickets for himself and his girlfriend, and she had been unable to go. It was Callas' last performance on the stage of an actual opera house, and though he later said he had found the evening overbearing and would not attend another opera for many years, Freddie retained a fondness for 'Vissi d'arte'—Callas' most requested piece—and once surprised his friend Montserrat Caballé by singing it all the way through, without making one mistake.

At the end of the Seventies, Freddie had developed a passion for the enigmatic German tenor, Fritz Wunderlich, who had died in Munich in 1966 following a fall, aged just thirty-five. Freddie and Barbara Valentin had visited Wunderlich's hunting-lodge and grave, just outside the city. In 1962, the tenor had sung the role of Tamino in Mozart's *The Magic Flute* for Radio Suisse Romand, in Lausanne, and singing opposite him had been a young Spanish soprano named Montserrat Caballé. Although this recording of his idols had never been commercially released, in 1980 Freddie had commissioned a copy of the tape from the Swiss radio station, and whilst raving over Wunderlich's magnificent voice, he had been no less impressed by the woman who, by the time he got to know her, was renowned the world over as 'La Superba'.

143

Montserrat told me about her first meeting with Freddie Mercury:

> It happened in New York, when I was there with Zubin Mehta, the conductor, singing Italian arias from Wagner. Freddie loved Wagner, so he came to the concert and asked to see me. He said, 'Hello, dear. I'm the singer from the group Queen. I'm a huge fan of your Norma, but I could never imagine you singing Wagner, so I had to hear for myself. I loved it!' Then he explained that he had heard me for the first time in Los Angeles, since which time he had come to several of my performances at the Royal Opera House in London, including my Tosca and Trovatore. I was very flattered. He knew absolutely everything there was to know about opera. He adored 'Lieberstod' from Wagner's Tristan and Isolde, and knew all the words. And you should have seen the videos he had at home—videos of me that I had never even seen myself! He was amazing!

Thirteen years Freddie's senior and from a poor background, Montserrat Caballé had worked in a handkerchief factory in her native Barcelona before being sponsored for a place in the Liceo Conservatoire. Her lucky break had occurred in 1965 when she had stood in for the indisposed Marilyn Horne in a performance of Donizetti's *Lucretia Borgia* at Carnegie Hall, since when she had sung to packed houses around the world. Then, a few years later she had almost died of cervical cancer and, shortly after her meeting with Freddie, there had been another trauma when, thinking herself to be suffering from no more than a bad dose of flu, she had checked into a New York hospital, only to be diagnosed as having a brain tumour, only to refuse surgery when informed that this was benign.

144

In August 1986, during Queen's visit to Barcelona, Freddie had submitted to a rare television interview on the top-rated arts magazine, *Informe Semenal*, and the presenter had asked him if he was interested in Spanish music and, if so, what type. Without hesitation he had declared himself a Caballé devotee, and had gone on to praise her formidable courage in the face of adversity. At the time of the interview, Montserrat was touring, but his comments were relayed to her by her brother Carlos, who was also her manager. Montserrat told me what had happened next:

> I was in Lausanne when I received a telephone call from the Mayor of Barcelona, asking me if I would sing something for the 1992 Olympics—something aimed at young people, as a means of attracting them to the city. 'Please don't sing any opera this time,' he told me, 'Sing something modern!' So I spoke to my brother, and Carlos said, 'Why don't we call Freddie Mercury? He's bound to have an idea what to do!' I agreed, Carlos approached him, and Freddie was so excited. He rented a suite at the Ritz Hotel in Barcelona, and we met him there in December 1986 when I returned from my tour. And you know, as soon as I entered that room I knew I was in the presence of a genius. He came so well prepared. So, we discussed our plans, he told me exactly what we would be doing, and we arranged an official business meeting so that the producer, Mike Moran, could be involved.

The meeting—the third between Freddie and his new friend and not the first, as has often been stated—took place over lunch in the same hotel on 27 March 1987. With Montserrat were Carlos Caballé and several members of her entourage, and with Freddie were Peter Freestone and Mike Moran, who told me:

145

Freddie and I wrote 'Exercises In Free Love' in my studio one night when we were both pissed. We'd done 'The Great Pretender', but we didn't have a B-side. So Freddie said, 'Oh, bugger it, just play something at the piano and we'll see what comes up!' It was three o'clock in the morning and—this is the absolute truth—he said, 'I'll pretend I'm a soprano like Montserrat Caballé!' Then he started warbling in this falsetto style, and we got the framework of the songs, which didn't sound bad. So, we decided to finish it off the next day when we were a bit more compos mentis. And now, at the Ritz in Barcelona, Freddie told her, 'I hope you're not offended by this, but this is me, pretending to be you. It's a bit of fun!' We played it, and she listened very carefully. Then she exclaimed, 'Is this for me? It's beautiful. I would really like to perform it—it will be given its world premiere next week at Covent Garden!' Then she turned to me and said, 'And you'll play the piano!'

Over the next few days Freddie and Moran virtually lived on their nerves, wondering what would happen when one of the world's greatest divas performed their song as her curtain-call for the cream of the social set. In fact, they had nothing to worry about. 'Exercises In Free Love' received a standing ovation.

Afterwards, at Garden Lodge, Freddie and Montserrat installed themselves at his grand piano for an impromptu recital of opera, jazz and gospel, which continued until dawn—by which time Montserrat had asked him to compose her a piece about her native city and Catalan heritage. She suggested several titles, most of them unpronouncable, but it was Freddie who proffered the simplest remedy: 'We'll have to call it "Barcelona", dear!'

Montserrat Caballé was regarded by devotees and the classical music world as considerably more professional within her art and her approach than any rock star could ever be. This proved Freddie's greatest challenge. Whereas he and his contemporaries often spent weeks in the studio perfecting and putting together a single track, artists of her calibre simply breezed in between concerts and more often than not completed the recording in one take. According to Mike Moran, however, there was the other side of the coin to be considered:

> To be fair, all that opera stars do is to read the printed page, which doesn't deviate that much. If you have a piece of Puccini, you can't change it and to be honest, if you've sung it ten times, you should be able to sing it again. With rock singers, its more instantly creative—they have the ability and the licence to change it. Freddie and I did all the work, composing and recording her part, which I wrote out for her. All she had to do was come in and sing it. But she loved working with Freddie, of course, because it gave her the opportunity to get away from the stuffiness of the opera world. And she was a very funny lady with such a great sense of humour.

The biggest problem facing the Mercury-Caballé partnership was that of availability. When she began working with Freddie in April 1987, she was heavily booked for another three years, which meant that he had to amend his schedule to accommodate what few spare dates she had. 'He was so very, very patient with me, and I appreciated that,' she said.

The fact that Montserrat had approached Freddie in the first place to propose this partnership, and not vice-versa, says a great deal for the enormous regard he had attracted from outside his own musical sphere—absolutely *no* other rock star (in the days before the likes of Pavarotti lowered their standards, to duet with artists sometimes so inferior, the end result defied description) would have dreamed of working with an operatic diva—at that time the concept of combining two such contrasting musical disciplines would have been declared tantamount to blasphemy by the opera world, and ridiculed by rock enthusiasts.

For Freddie, the consummate professional, a new era was about to begin which would enable his career to reach unprecedented heights and touch the hearts of an uncharted public. Were it not for the devastating news that he was about to receive, this new facet of his art would almost certainly have seen him working less and less with Queen, though Mike Moran is of the firm opinion that, even approaching middle age, Freddie would never have left the group entirely. 'Cliff Richard and Tina Turner, for instance, are doing stuff today as well as they ever did,' Moran said, adding, 'Freddie may have slightly *modified* his act, perhaps, but he would never have given up his work with Queen because this is what had made him.'

Montserrat recalled working with Freddie in the studio:

> He asked me what I thought of his voice, admitting that when young he had wanted to sing opera. His voice really was that of a baritone, though his fans would of course not have accepted that sort of voice. So, to prove a point, I got him to sing a duet with me–Violetta's and Germont's 'Dite alla giovine' from La Traviata, which I think was taped. He sang it very well. I don't know how much more opera he would have been able to do, though he was such a creative person. I'm sure he would have been able to improvise anything. The album itself was very well done. He and Mike Moran made such a good marriage between opera and rock, and it was very well produced. Freddie was a great practical joker—we both liked a laugh, though when we were working it was very

serious. And although we were sometimes working for hours at a time, we were never tired or bored. He would come into the studio and say, 'Look, my dear, I have another creation!' Then he would play 'La Japonaise', 'Guide Me Home', or 'The Fallen Priest', the most operatic piece on the album. Working with him was such an inspiration. I had so much respect for his workmanship.

Meanwhile, Freddie's private life took yet another savage and unexpected battering from the tabloids, and this time it was one of his closest, hitherto most respected friends who had effectively sold him down the river.

On 4 May 1987, almost the entire front page of the *Sun* was taken up with the headline alone: 'AIDS KILLS FREDDIE'S 2 LOVERS', beneath which were two photographs: one of Freddie hugging Tony Bastin, the other of he and John Murphy camping it up in women's hats. Inside the newspaper were further headlines: 'POP IDOL'S NIGHTMARE AS HIS GAY ORGIES RETURN TO HAUNT HIM' and '4 a.m. PHONE CALL OF TERROR'. Paul Prenter had lifted the lid completely off Freddie's private world. On 29 April, we now know, Freddie had called his personal assistant in the middle of the night and expressed his fears about dying of AIDS and, after some deliberation, Prenter had contacted a journalist friend and announced that he had a story that was 'white hot'. He had decided to reveal all about Freddie's affairs with Bastin, Murphy, and 'hundreds of homosexuals'. Stating that in all his nine years as the singer's right-hand man he had never once seen or heard of Freddie having a relationship with a woman, Prenter added, 'It was more likely that I would see him walk on water than go with a woman.'

Over the next few days, more revelations poured forth. At the end of the Seventies Freddie had assured James Johnson of the *Evening Standard*, 'We're probably the straightest band around. For instance, we were always anti-drugs from the start. We went through all that in our teens, and we never felt that good music comes from being high.' Now, Prenter spoke of Freddie's alleged cocaine binges with David Bowie and Rod Stewart, and of how he and Brian May had often sneaked into the wings during Queen's concerts to snort the drug, of how his one and only collaboration with Michael Jackson had been aborted when Jackson had caught him out in his studio, and of how Freddie and Kenny Everett had abruptly ended their friendship after a violent quarrel. 'Kenny had a great capacity for cocaine, but not for paying for it,' Prenter said, 'He accused Freddie of taking all his coke, but it was actually the other way round.'

Worst of all, perhaps, was the grossly and cruelly misleading picture-spread which appeared in the *Sun* on 7 May, headlined, 'ALL THE QUEEN'S MEN'. 'Freddie Mercury likes men who look as if they can eat a lorry for breakfast,' the editorial ran. Prenter, now described as the singer's *former* personal manager, had opened his private photograph album.

Freddie was depicted stripped to the waist with 'bristly' Big Vince, the perfect American who had refused to relocate to England—with 'snuggly' Winnie Kirkenberger and 'campy' Peter Straker—with 'matey' John Reid and, more suitably attired with 'zany' Michael Jackson and 'cokey' Rod Stewart. For good measure, the newspaper threw in a shot of the man Freddie had always wanted but never got around to even meeting—Burt Reynolds. Confessing how Freddie always went weak at the knees every time he saw the actor's photograph, Prenter added, 'Freddie liked his men big, muscular and rugged, with short hair and a moustache. Burt Reynolds fitted the bill perfectly. Freddie thought he was wonderful, gorgeous. If Burt had walked into the room, I'm sure Freddie would have fainted.'

Freddie hit the roof. 'Paul Prenter wasn't a *horrible* person,' David Evans emphasised. 'He was an easy-going, simple Irish guy. He worked hard and he was passionate about the recording business. He was part of the circus, and when those wheels get rolling they often roll people under them.' Now, not only did Prenter lose an extremely well-paid job, he lost Freddie's friendship and the respect of almost every one of his friends. Freddie also amended his will: had Prenter remained loyal and kept his mouth shut, he would soon have become a wealthy man. Several times over the next few years he would attempt to worm his way back into Freddie's affections, claiming that Richard Ellis of the *Sun* had hounded him into selling him his story, but always to no avail. Not that Freddie had heard the last of Prenter, by any means.

In order to cope with the burden of his problems and troubled state of mind, Freddie hurled himself back into his latest project. His work with Montserrat Caballé was extremely demanding. Because of her bulging diary of commitments, her vocal sections for the album were recorded on tape by Freddie, singing in a curious *mélange* of counter-tenor and coloratura—something he did inoirdinately well—then forwarded to her wherever she was appearing. Their first complete song was 'Barcelona', quickly followed by Freddie's and Mike Moran's 'The Fallen Priest', which they had written in collaboration with Tim Rice. The first time Rice listened to these and their companion masterpiece, 'The Golden Boy', in their finished, polished versions, he could only rue the fact that Freddie had never had an opera composed for him. 'Puccini rather than Wagner,' he lamented. 'Freddie was way, way ahead of his time where opera was concerned.' Montserrat told the press at the time, 'As an opera singer, my voice is an instrument in the hands of the composer. Working with Freddie, my *special* composer, my voice feels free for the first time!'

The pair had great fun working together, the more they got to know each other. Montserrat had a wacky sense of humour and was not stuck up as many opera stars are reputed to be. She relished Freddie's ribald jokes, and was never offended by his language. According to Jim Hutton, the first words she spoke in Garden Lodge—after she tripped over a loose carpet—were, 'Oh, shit!' David Evans recounted an amusing anecdote concerning one of Montserrat Caballé's more unusual gifts to her friend:

> Montsy didn't quite know what to send Freddie as a thank you present for working with her. Then one day one of her operatic costumes arrived in the post. I think it was the one she'd worn some years before when she'd played Juliet. And what do you do with a dress? You have to display it! So Freddie put it on some sort of form to fill it out, and it was placed inside a glass case and hung halfway up one of the huge piers in his drawing-room so that everybody could see it. It certainly was a conversation piece!

'Barcelona', the pair's most celebrated and challenging rock-opera-symphonic *chef-d'oeuvre*, was premiered on 30 May before an invited audience of 6,000 at the Ku Club, an infamous society night spot in San Antonio, on the island of Ibiza. The extravaganza was to promote *Expo '92*, the 500th anniversary of America, and most importantly Barcelona's hosting of the 1992 Olympics, for which the song was to be the official anthem. There were also contributions from many international stars, including Duran Duran, Harrison Ford, Diego Maradona, Chris Rea, Roman Polanski and Spandau Ballet, and it was televised throughout most of the world. South Africa was one of the few exceptions, though the plight of that country was referred to when a singer named Nona Hendrix dedicated a song, 'Winds Of

152

Change', to Nelson Mandela—before diving into the pool and hitting her head on the bottom, which earned her several stitches and a waspish comment from Freddie, 'It's a pity they didn't stitch up her mouth *before* she sang!'

Closing the evening before a scintillating backdrop of multicoloured fountains and fireworks—one which was partially recreated in David Mallett's excellent video, aided by some 300 fans holding disposable cigarette lighters—Freddie wore a fetching blue dress-suit and cummerbund, and Montserrat a sparkling, voluminous gown for what Tim de Lisle described as, 'An exercise in high camp, with two of the world's most distinguished practitioners vying to see who could go furthest over the top.' The standing ovation after 'Barcelona', not surprising considering the location, lasted almost as long as the song.

Freddie told the coterie of press—probably unaware that most of them were blind to their combined talents and more interested in lampooning them for Freddie's arch-campness and Montserrat's size—'I defy any other rock 'n' roll personality to duet with a legendary opera diva, and survive!' The flamboyant statement only provoked the media into penning a series of so-called reviews which, besides being dismissive of one of the finest pieces either star had ever recorded, were virulently offensive. Both singers seriously considered suing *Melody Maker* and the *New Musical Express*—but decided not to when they realized that the adverse publicity was working in their favour. The single, released at the end of October 1987, reached Number 8 in the British charts, and made the Top Ten all over Europe. In Spain, a country which did not favour singles, the entire 20,000 pressing sold out in just three hours.

Ibiza was also the setting for Freddie's forty-first birthday party in September. Of the 400 guests, eighty were close friends flown in from Heathrow on a chartered DC9, then transported in a fleet of taxis to Pykes, one of the Island's most exclusive hotels, where the Olympics Committee had organized a sumptuous bash with flamenco dancers, a fireworks display spelling Freddie's name in huge letters, and a ten-foot cake decorated with the opening lines of 'Barcelona'. Freddie was dispondent when he learned that Montserrat Caballé could not be there because she was giving a recital in Stockholm, though she did sing 'Happy Birthday' down the telephone.

Freddie's continuing involvement with Montserrat, along with Roger Taylor's extra-curricular activities, fuelled more rumours that Queen were about to split. Taylor had formed The Cross, with himself as vocalist. 'Of course Queen haven't split up,' he told *Kerrang!* 'But the band has had a good run over the last couple of years, and we all decided that we would shup up for a couple of years and give people a rest, especially the brainless idiots of Radio One who are probably sick of having to play Queen singles for the past fifteen years, or whatever!' Freddie observed in a radio interview:

> We could all just go away and say we've had enough and live happily ever after, but I don't think that's what we're in. We're in it to make music, and what else can I do? This is the thing that interests me most. You don't know what it means when you write a song that people actually appreciate and they say it's a good song. It's a wonderful feeling! We've all had ego problems, but we've never let it go that far where we've actually said forget it, because the four of us have this chemistry that's worked so well for us. So why kill the goose that lays the golden egg? We will just carry on until one of us drops dead, or something, or is just replaced. I think if I suddenly left, they'd have the mechanism to replace me. Not easy to replace, ha!

154

The Cross released numerous singles and three albums, none of which sold well, though one of their songs, 'Heaven For Everyone' with Freddie on vocals, was revived with tremendous success by Queen some years later. It is said, however, that Freddie only worked with the ensemble out of loyalty to Roger Taylor, and that he disliked the other members of The Cross. Jim Hutton later recalled their rowdy, slobbish behaviour at one of Freddie's birthday parties, and his comment, 'What a pain they were. They're never coming here again.'

Brian May's projects, for the time being, were even less commendable. Anita Dobson had had a huge hit in 1986 with May's production of 'Anyone Can Fall In Love', the theme from *Eastenders* which was little more than a novelty number. The critics were unanimous in stating that she was a far better actress than she would ever be a singer, and forecast great things when she signed to star opposite former pop star Adam Faith in the stage-musical version of his television hit-series, *Budgie*. Dobson's other work with Brian May was unbelievably dire, though there was much worse to come when one of the finest rock musicians of all time teamed up with the spoof group Bad News—an outfit comprising alternative comedians Ade Edmondson, Peter Richardson, Rick Mayall and Nigel Planer from television's *The Comic Strip* which certainly lived up to its name. 'Get Your Hands Round A 12-Inch Now!' screamed the publicity posters for their debut album. 'Brian was head-over-heels in love with Anita, and he allowed this to cloud his professional judgement,' a Queen spokesman told me. 'And Bad News' rendition of "Bohemian Rhapsody", with John and Roger caterwauling all the "Gallileos", was nothing short of sacrilege. Freddie *pretended* to accept what they'd done, but in reality he was furious and wanted to punch Brian's lights out.'

One doubts that Freddie ever thought of such a thing, let alone said it. When told that there was no evading the fact that, from a commercial angle and owing to a lack of public performances, Queen's popularity appeared to be on the wane—more so in the United States, where some radio stations no longer played their records—Freddie told his favourite journalist, David Wigg of the *Daily Express*, 'There are no plans to take on a grand tour at the moment, but we are *still* working together. Just wait and see!'

The fans were placated by the release of three videos. *Queen: The Magic Years* was directed by Rudi Dolezal and Hannes Rossacher, 'The Torpedo Twins', and documented the group's story with rare concert footage, glimpses of them working, laughing and cursing in the studio, and anecdotes from friends and colleagues. Small sections of the films were downright gratuitous, such as nonsensical comments from racing-driver Jackie Stewart, Status Quo, and a handful of comparatively unimportant pop stars who giggled and fidgeted and did not seem to know where they were and why they were being filmed. Elton John also made several cameo appearances, courting media mockery by annoyingly referring to Freddie as 'she'.

It is now known that Freddie had held back during his in-depth interview with David Wigg over his HIV test—the fact that only days before speaking to the journalist the results of this and a subsequent test had confirmed the worst. Not only was Freddie HIV positive, he quite likely had already developed full-blown AIDS. Wigg therefore must be excused for posing a question which had been asked many times, long before there had been any rumours of Freddie being unwell: What would happen to his vast antiques collection after his death? Freddie must really have put on a brave face to respond, jokingly, 'I want to be *buried* with all my treasures, like the Pharoahs. If I can afford it, I'll have a pyramid built in Kensington. Now wouldn't *that* be fab?'

156

David Wigg and many others who were reasonably close to Freddie, though not close enough to know all the details, did of course have their suspicions concerning his health. Wigg confessed, 'It was very difficult for me. I feared something may have been wrong when I met him at his birthday party in Ibiza, but couldn't be sure because he was in such a good mood.' The first person Freddie confided in about his illness was Montserrat Caballé, who choked back the tears as she told me:

> Freddie was not a coward, and he was not afraid of facing up to the truth that his life was in danger. He didn't know how to tell his friends and family, but he was honest with me from the very beginning. There is no reason why he should have told me and not anyone else—save that he knew I could be discreet—but he wanted to tell me, and I listened. To be honest, when he said he wanted to confide in me, I just thought he wanted to tell me, privately, how much he had enjoyed working with me. I never expected that...

The next ones to be told about Freddie's condition were Mary Austin, Joe Fanelli, Jim Beach, and Jim Hutton who recalled, 'He never liked talking about his illness. From that moment, if anything came on the television to do with AIDS, we would turn over to another channel or switch the set off. It's not that he was unsympathetic towards others with the illness, he simply didn't like being reminded of his fate.' Freddie also confided in Roger Taylor's girlfriend, Dominique, when she told him that she had breast cancer. For the time being, the other members of Queen were told nothing.

David Wigg had flown to Ibiza for Freddie's last birthday bash —not in his journalist capacity, but as a friend, though he *had* interviewed Freddie and Montserrat about their project. Freddie, however, was unhappy with the result of this particular interview, declaring, 'I gave him cream, and all he prints is sour milk.' There was, however, more to it than this, as Wigg explained:

> Freddie never knew what a battle I had trying to get the piece in because the editor and deputy editor of the Express had got so used to my having access to Freddie that they got a little blasé about his star status. So I asked them for five minutes of their time, and played them the 'Barcelona' video. I told them that the record would be huge. The deputy editor loved opera—he'd never seen a rock star performing that kind of material before, and that's what made them print the interview. Otherwise they wouldn't have printed anything, and Freddie would have gone mad!

Aware that time was probably running out, Freddie tried to ignore his occasional fatigue and set-backs by plunging himself into a number of projects that were not directly connected with his music. The rest of 1987 was almost exclusively devoted to putting his personal affairs in order, ensuring that those friends and lovers, past and present, who were looking after him now would be taken care of after his death. He purchased the Mews, a pair of houses in Logan Mews, the tiny street next to Garden Lodge which had once been annexed to the house. Converted into a single residence by the Hoare family, the asking price was now a very steep £275,000. Freddie saw the owner just twice: once to clinch the deal and demand immediate vacant possession, and again to hand over the cheque for the full amount with a jocular but firm, 'Here's your money, dear. Now please fuck off!'

Freddie lavished as much attention on his new property as he had on Garden Lodge, spending over £100,000 on renovations and even personally designing a twin-domed conservatory which was to be erected next to it. 'Freddie had many things to achieve before his illness caught up with him,' Jim Hutton said. 'He wanted to leave a little bit of paradise on earth.' Freddie stocked up his pool with £12,000-worth of Koi carp. Later in the year, when some of them became ill, he spent a small fortune on specialist veterinary treatment.

Early in January 1988, Queen entered the Townhouse Studios to begin recording *The Miracle*. The healthy in-group squabbles were still there, essential for every album. Freddie recalled:

> We went into the studio very hungry. After two years we really wanted to record again. You have to fight. If it was made too easy for me, I would come up with lesser material. Because we fight, it becomes much more interesting and you get la creme de la creme. The fighting for the Queen songs has been one of the worthwhile factors. Some of the ones that were discarded ended up on my solo album. They're good, ha-ha-ha!

The press were less interested in the album than in Queen's personal lives. Only John Deacon escaped as the tabloids served up hefty portions about Freddie's allegedly failing health, Brian May's denials that he and Anita Dobson were an item, and Roger Taylor's involvement with Debbie Leng, the girl in the suggestive Cadbury's Flake television commercial. Taylor had been dating the pretty model, sixteen years his junior, for a few months, since she had appeared in one of The Cross' videos. What many were unable to comprehend was the unorthodox manner in which he went about making their relationship more permanent—marrying his long-time girlfriend, Dominique Beyrand, on 25 January with Freddie and Mary Austin signing the register as witnesses and apparently deserting her three weeks later to move into the £700,000 house he had purchased for Debbie Leng and himself.

159

Taylor informed the press that he and Dominique were undergoing a trial separation, while his mother told the *People*, 'The wedding was a love pact because the pair knew their relationship was doomed.' It was David Wigg who broke the exclusive for the *Daily Express*, drawing the confession from Taylor, 'I wanted to make a commitment to Dominique and our two children. I wanted to make my children legal and secure. Dominique is a terrific woman. We really are the best of friends.'

The press were also remarkably expedient with their revelations about Leng's past life, claiming that for one so young she had already enjoyed romantic liaisons with five top rock stars, including David Essex and David Bowie, though it was her most recent involvement with the American pop star Simon Climie (of the duo Climie Fisher) which caused her the most hassle a few months later at the Montreux Festival, when Climie and Taylor squared up to each other in the bar of the Hyatt Continental Hotel, and almost came to blows. A spokesman for Taylor attempted to deny that the clash had taken place—unaware that photographs of it had already appeared in the press, along with Climie's complaint about Taylor's 'attitude' and bad language. Freddie found the situation hilarious, and told friends, 'I only wish I could have been there. While they were at it, handbags at thirty paces, I'd have run off with that gorgeous Simon and you wouldn't have seen me for dust!'

On 14 April, Freddie appeared alongside Cliff Richard in a special charity performance of *Time*—all the proceeds were donated to the Terrence Higgins Trust, the organization set up in 1982 and named as a tribute to the first known British AIDS victim, to provide information and support for fellow sufferers. Naturally this set the tongues wagging regarding Freddie's own health, particularly when he was observed to have lost a little weight—nothing as yet related to his condition, but on account of him recently adopting a stricter diet and cutting down on his vodka intake.

Freddie's secret almost certainly would have been revealed, however, had it not been for the preventive action taken by one of his friends, a well-known British singer and former one-night stand who spent some time with him before and after the charity performance, and who specifically requested not to be named:

> I was in Freddie's dressing-room. We'd had a few drinks and I was straightening his collar when I noticed a large, dark blotch on one side of his face. He said it was a bruise and that he'd bumped into something at home. I knew otherwise because I'd seen this sort of thing before. Freddie allowed me to cover it with a dab of make-up, then he told me he had AIDS. I was very upset, but he seemed to take it very calmly. He shrugged his shoulders and said, 'It's just one of those things, dear. We've all got to go some time!' Then he swore at me for fussing over him! Two months later when I met him in Munich, he had more blotches on his arms and neck, and I instinctively knew that this was the beginning of the end.

A few days after the *Time* performance, Freddie flew to Madrid to surprise Montserrat Caballé, who was celebrating twenty-five years in opera with a royal gala at the city's Opera House. As with her recital at Covent Garden, her 'Freddie songs'—by this time an integral part of almost every soirée—were sung at the end of her performance, and it was Freddie who walked on to the stage during her curtain-call to present her with the biggest bouquet she had ever seen in her life.

Montserrat Caballé was not the only *grande dame* in Freddie's professional life at this time. At the beginning of the year he had been approached by Britain's top musical-stage star, Elaine Paige,

161

who was interested in recording an album of Queen songs. Freddie had known Elaine since 1986—she had visited Garden Lodge several times and had frequently turned up at his birthday parties with her then partner, Tim Rice. Freddie had loved her definitive portrayal of Eva Perón, and regarded her as 'The English Piaf –which is sad, considering he never lived to see her in Pam Gems' *Piaf*, one of her greatest triumphs and the definitive role many believed she had been born to play.

Produced by the ubiquitous Mike Moran, who conducted the New Philharmonic Orchestra on six of the ten songs, *Elaine Paige: The Queen Album* was an innovation, introducing the group's work to a new audience. Freddie would have loved to have sat in on the recording sessions, declaring, 'I like to add my two-penneth, dear!' Moran, however, allowed him access to the studio just once. 'Elaine was putting the vocal on, and all Freddie did was hold us all up for about three hours,' he told me, 'So I said, "Well, okay. We've had a nice time, now you'd better piss off and let us get on with some work!"'

The end result of these sessions was breathtaking. Few serious critics would disagree that when a *chanteuse* of Paige's ability attempts material which they themselves have not created, that material invariably becomes their personal property. Her interpretations of three Queen numbers in particular—'Who Wants To Live Forever', 'Love Of My Life' and 'Is This The World We Created'—are without any doubt technically superior to Queen's originals, and 'Radio Ga-Ga' almost so. One may only lament that there was never a *Queen Album II*.

On 8 October, Freddie and Montserrat Caballé appeared in their most glittering spectacular—again in front of the Spanish royal family—topping the bill at 'La Nit', a huge open-air festival in Barcelona's Montjuich Park. Here, in aid of the International Red Cross, 150,000 fans celebrated the 'Portico', or four-year run-up to the Olympics, which included the ceremonial arrival of

162

the flag from the games' last venue, Seoul. The bill boasted such stalwarts as Dionne Warwick, Earth Wind & Fire, Spandau Ballet, José Carreras, Rudolph Nureyev and Jerry Lew Lewis, and there was an amusing moment when the dreadlocked singer Eddy Grant took to the stage—and the royals left their box until he had finished. Freddie and Montserrat eclipsed them all—with 'Barcelona', and two songs from the *Barcelona* album, scheduled for release two days later: 'The Golden Boy' and 'How Can I Go On'. The thirty-five musicians accompanying them, directed by Mike Moran, had been flown over from London at Freddie's expense, and joined forces with the Barcelona Opera House Orchestra & Choir. To say the evening ended on a majestic note was indeed an understatement.

Then pair were however severely criticized for miming –the reason for this having nothing to do with a throat infection, as Freddie stated. Most of the audience might even not have known they were miming, had someone had the sense to provide them with dummy microphones—and had it not been for the sudden slowing down of the playback tape halfway through the performance. Despite his powerful voice as a rock star, when attempting to sing live with a trained operatic soprano—as opposed to having their separately recorded voices blended by studio technicians—Freddie would have been drowned by both the orchestra and his partner. Also, when the pair were seen in close-up on the television screen, their lip-synchs were nothing short of preposterous—hardly surprising, for Montserrat had never been expected to mime in her life, and Freddie had only done so under duress for the Montreux Pop Festival and the odd appearance on *Top of the Pops*.

The press had a field-day, with Adrian Deevoy of *Q* supplying the most amusingly accurate description of a legend who, in his eyes, had failed to fulfil his duty. Deevoy—who had been given a personal backstage pass from Freddie, only to receive short shrift

163

from the same armed security guard who initially refused admittance to Master of Ceremonies, Mike Moran!—wrote:

> So what must we do in order to meet Frederick Bulsara, the man for whom the word 'ludicrous' has never been adequate? The unblushing frontperson of Queen who attempted to marry Madame Butterfly to Led Zeppelin while wearing a pink feather boa, having apparently secreted several pounds of root vegetables down his ballet tights. Here he is, the wrist-flicking pianist and melodramatic lyricist whom even Beelzebub couldn't stand the sight of. The macho-mustachioed bon viveur who could never decide whether to toss roses to his adoring fans or show them his bottom.

In fact, Deevoy *was* granted an interview, albeit a brief one, the next day at the Royal Opera House in Covent Garden. The occasion was a lunch-time party to launch the *Barcelona* album—a brilliant concept which, like the single, the music press hated to a man. 'In those days, the press didn't know what to make of it,' Mike Moran said. 'Later, of course, opera became big time with Pavarotti, the World Cup and the Three Tenors. So suddenly, everybody wants to duet with an opera singer. Yet again, Freddie was courageous and before his time.'

Deevoy's question, as to why Freddie was smoking in view of his alleged throat infection, was met with an archetypically theatrical, "Oh, do fuck off, dear!' The interviews, unfortunately for one usually so adept, was conducted with exactly the same boring questions that Freddie and Montserrat had been asked dozens of times already, and attracted the same by now lethargic responses. Once again, Freddie vowed never to speak to the British press again—and so far as is known, he never did.

—'I defy any other rock 'n' roll personality to duet with a
legendary opera diva, and survive! (IC)

Nine: Praying For A Miracle

As the New Year dawned it was not Freddie, but Brian May, who hogged the tabloids with the "sensational" news of his split from his wife of thirteen years, Chrissie, so that he could be with Anita Dobson. '£1 m For The Love Of Angie', yelled the opening blast in the *Sunday Mirror*, voicing the hacks' assumption that the British public knew only the names of the characters in its soap-operas, and not the actors/actresses who played them. From then on, each exclsuive divulged how the guitarist had allegedly spent £1 million on a 'farewell' Christmas present—a six-roomed house—for his heartbroken wife. And of course there was the obligatory 'family friend' who occasionally stepped forward to add a juicy tidbit and sympathise with May's 'torn feelings'.

On the musical side, May suffered further humiliation by not only attending Bad News' dreadful gig at the London Marquee, but by getting on to the stage with fellow guitar legend, Jeff Beck, and jamming with this tripe. Earlier, the ensemble had hurled a bucket of water into the audience—to be rewarded by a sudden deluge of pint pots filled with urine. For once, Andrew Smith of *Melody Maker* may have been justified in commenting, 'However hard Bad News might try, they will never be as absurd as the real thing.'

The May-Dobson relationship—eventually, they would marry—seemed to have more ups and downs than the proverbial rollercoaster. On the eve of the premiere of *Budgie*, the press reported that the couple had gone their separate ways because May, unable to cope with not seeing his children on a regular basis, had opted to return to his wife. A few weeks later they were together again at May's Berkshire home, with Dobson lamenting the premature closure of her musical at a loss of over £1 million—and May consoling her with a £42,000 red Mercedes

500 SL convertible. Speaking of the severe depression caused by personal problems, the guitarist opened his heart to Jeff Moses of the American magazine *RIP*, saying bitterly, "We've been sheltered. We never had this tabloid thing going on in the past. It's the most awful experience. They just want the dirt. They don't want to know about making music, they want to know if you've been screwing someone else's wife.'

Freddie was ecstatic. For once the press were leaving *him* alone. Not even when his 'new look' photograph appeared in the *Sunday Times* did the media cotton on to the fact that he had grown his short, stubbly beard to camouflage the lines of illness and the Kaposi's Sarcoma blotches, just beginning to show on his face. 'I just couldn't be bothered to shave any more. It's as boring as slicing bread,' he confessed in the brief editorial.

There was considerable media interest in Freddie's latest foible—a 144-piece dinner service which had taken ten months collect, and which had set him back a staggering £250,000! Each pieces—from the £2,000 coffee cups to the £5,100 tureen—was hand-painted with miniature copies of Constable masterpieces, edged with gold filigree. One week after purchasing this, Freddie and Jim Hutton flew to Geneva, where they spent two days studying the art of porcelain painting with a master of the medium, Shira Misrez, before returning to Garden Lodge with four Misrez pieces, for which Freddie had shelled out £10,000.

What really shocked Queen's fans at this time was the announcement that they would not be touring to promote the new album: though the rest of the group were keen to hit the road again, Freddie was not. The tour should have taken in uncharted territories such as China and Russia, but placing particular emphasis on the United States, where they had not had a sizeable hit for five years. Two years later, speaking to the *Daytona Daily News*, Brian May conceded that the Americans could have been put off by the drastic change in Freddie's appearance: 'As soon as he cut his hair, that alienated people. People sometimes don't know where we're coming from.' He may of course have been making a guarded reference to the country's increasing homophobia in the wake of the AIDS epidemic—and the fact that had it not been for Freddie's arch campness, itself linked to his sexuality, Queen would never have made it to begin with.

Realising that the American tabloids might pick up on his changed physical appearance and use this as a weapon against him, as was happening in Britain, Freddie emphasised in a telephone conversation with Sally Stratton of *Music & Me*: '*I'm* the one who doesn't want to tour, dear. *I* want to change this cycle that we've been going through for so long. If we *do* tour, I want to do it for totally different reasons. I've had enough of these bombastic lights and staging effects. I don't thing a forty-two-year-old man should be running around in his leotard any more!' These views would be reiterated on 29 May when, in 'Queen For An Hour', the group's first collective radio interview in almost a decade, they spoke to Mike Reid of Radio One.

Queen's début single from their forthcoming *The Miracle* album, 'I Want It All', was released on 2 May 1989. It reached Number 3 in the British charts, and though a relative flop in America, it earned the group the vital air-play which had been lacking in parts of the country for some time. As another mighty studio anthem, it was a big hit across Europe—particularly in Germany, where the video was premiered on a massive screen at half-time during the UEFA Cup Final between Napoli and Stuttgart. With its over-use of huge Xenon Trouper stadium spotlights only exaggerating Freddie's bloated appearance, this film was bland by Queen's usual standards. The song itself, otherwise, was a fine one and like all the others on the album accredited to all four members of the group—'So there will be no falling out who gets the most royalties. Now isn't *that* a good idea!' Freddie told one interviewer—though in some of the other numbers on the album it is not difficult to ascertain which individual member of the group had influenced them. And not so very long before he had actually commended this individuality, saying in a radio interview, 'The trademark of Queen which I like just happens to be a coincidence that there are four writers who write very different material, which gives us maybe a wider span than most other groups.'

Freddie's reluctance to tour was linked by the European press to his still only alleged physical condition. It was Roger Taylor who was asked the first direct question regarding this—'Evil voices claim that Freddie has AIDS. Is this true?'—by a German reporter, Gotz Kuhnmund, while Taylor and Brian May were promoting the new album in Munich. No sensible journalist would have posed so insensitive a question, let alone anticipated an affirmative response, and the drummer was justifiably defensive of his friend:

> What stupidity! Freddie is as healthy as ever and sings better than ever on the new album. We had a party at Brian's a few days ago, and Freddie didn't exactly give the impression that he was on his death bed. The reason we're not going to tour is because we can't agree on the whole process. Everything else is just a stupid rumour!

According to Jim Hutton, it was at around this time that Freddie told the rest of the group that he was seriously ill, though it is not known if the actual word 'AIDS' came up in the conversation when, in a Montreux restaurant, Hutton claimed, 'Freddie rolled up his right trouser leg and raised his leg to the table to let the others see the painful, open wound weeping on the side of his calf.' Hutton concluded, 'I think the band had all been aware that Freddie was seriously ill, and his leg that night was the confirmation they had all been expecting.'

169

One of his closest friends, the singer who had observed his Kaposi's Sarcoma for the first time, confirmed that Freddie had broken the sad news to the other members of Queen while in Montreux, but dismissed the 'leg-on-table' incident, saying:

> Freddie would never have done anything so crude. It just wasn't his style. And in a restaurant of all places? No, I don't think so! The truth is, he got the band together and said very quietly, 'I suppose you all know what I'm dealing with?' The word AIDS was never used. It wasn't necessary, for their worst fears had already been confirmed by the way he looked, the way he'd been losing weight. Now, of course, they realized that they would eventually lose a very dear friend, and worse still they realized that their future was in jeopardy too. They were terrified of coming to terms with the fact that without Freddie, they would be absolutely nothing, that they would become just another defunct group, which of course has been proved.

The Miracle, Queen's sixteenth album, was better received than anything the group had done in the last decade, and housed in their most appealing cover yet–a computerized four-in-one shot of their blended faces, sharing five eyes and an asymetric haircut. Even the British music press did not disapprove of this chart-topper, though Freddie still burned their reviews. After all the harm and gratuitous insults these people had inflicted in the past, it was too late to redress the balance now. "If the clipping was from a British publication, it went straight onto the fire," the aforementioned singer friend said, "The American and European clippings, he kept."

In America, the album was looked upon as a revelation. 'Mercury has *never* sounded better,' observed *Rolling Stone* while

Music Express called it, 'A breathless, frenetic burst of pure energy which takes more twists and turns than a run through the Indy 500.' Brian May told the magazine, 'I think we'd all die happy if we could just conquer North America again.' The anonymous scribe for *Tracks* wrote, 'Queen are the sort of band who are always there, like buses or the weather. Everyone from American teenagers to German double-glazing salesmen in their forties has either owned a Queen record, seen them play, or behaved foolishly to one of their singles at a disco.'

Maura Sutton, writing for *RAW*, singled out Freddie for particular praise, and also hit out at the British music press for its continuous persecution of him: 'Freddie Mercury has always attracted the greatest amount of flak from critics too busy crawling up their own posteriors to recognize the man's tongue-in-cheek self-deprecating witticisms, or to acknowledge the fact that he's one of the greatest rock vocalists *ever*.' The review which excited Freddie the most, however, was the one penned by Chris Welch in *Metal Hammer*, which issued a stern warning to any would-be contenders for the Queen crown:

> First there came rock groups. And lo, they were good. And then came Queen, and the world trembled. For Queen are not just a group, they are a way of life, an institution, and they have a place in the national heritage of treasures that means they now transcend all current fashions and styles...

Such enthusiasm—and the fact that it was a brilliant album—enabled *The Miracle* to reach Number 24 in the American charts, and again brought up the subject of a possible tour, which drew the sharp but jocular quip from Roger Taylor, 'The demand for us to tour is getting to be a pain in the arse!' Brian May was more indignant when speaking to Chris Welch—

this time writing for *Insight*: 'Freddie just doesn't *want* to tour, so taking the touring side of things away has really messed up my life—without any exaggeration. I feel it's taken the whole balance out of my life.'

In the end, Queen's fans had to make do with a video, albeit an excellent one. *Rare Live: A Concert Through Time & Space* offered a panorama of the group's on-stage activities over the last sixteen years, and was principally aimed at those younger fans who had not been there to witness their formative years. Their next single, taken from the album and released on 19 June, was 'Breakthru', a fine, bouncy song for which the group demanded an extra-special video—and a costly one, for they insisted on the shoot taking place atop a speeding train. This of course was easier said than done, though the first stage of the problem was effectively solved by hiring the privately owned Nene Valley Railway, in Cambridgeshire, for two days. An old stream train was then 'Queened up' by having its front and side plates fitted and emblazoned with *The Miracle Express*. Even the lumps of coal were painted red and gold!

Initially, the railway company refused to allow Queen to be filmed on top of the train while it was actually moving, suggesting that the speeding of the vehicle could be effected by using a separate backdrop, as had happened in some of the old Hollywood movies. This idea they found bland, so a compromise was reached. The group insured themselves and their entourage, including Debbie Leng, for £2 million, forking out a staggering £150,000 for the premium. This, added to the £200,000 production costs and the £30,000 customising fee for the train, resulted in 'Breakthru' becoming one of the most expensive videos ever made.

The filming took place with *The Miracle Express* hurtling away at 60 mph on straight stretches of track, putting the fear of God into Freddie who, like the others was prevented from falling off only by a rickety-looking iron rail. Afterwards, for the benefit of fans and photographers who had been tipped off about the secret location by Radio Cambridge, he joked, 'For one moment back there, I thought I'd cashed in my chips!' Asked why he had chosen Debbie Leng, against Roger Taylor's wishes, he replied, 'Because I wanted to make a *sexy* video. And who better to do it than Debbie!' The single reached Number 7 in the charts, and its successor, 'The Invisible Man', peaked at Number 12, though the next two singles—'Scandal' and 'The Miracle' itself—did not fare quite so well, just failing to get into the Top Twenty.

Of the videos for these three songs, the one for 'The Miracle' was the most interesting. The group, only wishing to appear at the end of the film, hit on the novelty idea that each of them would be substituted by a junior 'lookalike' wearing identical costumes. Auditions were held at several London stage schools, and four boys aged between ten and fourteen were chosen from an opening list of 500—a difficult task, for not only were the boys' looks of paramount importance, their miming and impersonation skills had to be spot-on. 'It's Freddie & The Schoolboy Dreamers!' proclaimed one publication, printing photographs of 'John' (James Currie), 'Roger' (Adam Gladdish), 'Brian' (Paul Howard) and 'Freddie' (Ross McCall), posing with the real Queen. Said Freddie of his double, whose previous thespian experience included a spell on the West End stage in *Les Misérables* and the role of the Artful Dodger in a touring production of *Oliver!*, 'The resemblance is frightening. Was *I* really *that* good?'

In early August, the artists involved with *Live Aid* were asked to pose in Piccadilly's Trocadero leisure complex for inclusion in the Madame Tussaud's waxworks museum. While everyone else posed for their models in person, Freddie sent a portfolio of photographs, worried about anyone getting too close up to him in case they began speculating about his appearance. He had started to lose weight, and often felt tired and unwell. He hit the tabloid headlines again early in November 1989, when the *Sunday Mirror* declared, 'Gay Freddie To Be A "Dad"'. The editorial then went on to explain how Mary Austin was pregnant by an interior designer she refused to name (subsequently revealed to be Piers Cameron), and that Freddie had struck up an amazing love-pact to become a 'father' to the child after telling Mary, 'I love you, but I can't *make* love to you!' Some time before he is alleged to have told a friend, 'A baby? I'd rather have another cat, my dear!' And now, there was another obligatory 'friend' to tell all:

> Mary is fond of the real father but she has no intention of living with him. The main consideration was having a baby. Freddie was always jealous that the rest of the guys in the group had families. He's not at all jealous that Mary went with this other man. They are madly in love, but they are not possessive physically. It was heartbreaking for her when Freddie told her he could not hide his homosexuality any longer, but she has never complained.

The feature, typically, was complemented with a photograph of the couple, captioned, 'Gay Godfather—Freddie With Girlfriend Mary'. That same week, Brian May's girlfriend featured in the press—Anita Dobson's most recent project, the otherwise excellent television situation comedy *Split Ends*, was about to be axed after just one series. Set in a hairdressing salon, this original, very funny show contained a contribution from Freddie when, to the tune of 'Funiculi-Funicula', one of the characters had been stopped in his tracks while belting out, 'Whip me, Strip me, Tie me to a tree, Spank me, Wank me, Shoot all over me!'

For Freddie, sadly, there were now far too many days when he was feeling exhausted and ill, and adding to his personal distress was the palpable strain of keeping his tragic secret from the rest of the world. He was regularly visiting his Harley Street specialist, Gordon Atkinson, and when he told Freddie to stop smoking, he did so in a single stroke—quite a feat, for he had been smoking up to forty cigarettes a day since the age of sixteen. The smile, the spirit and the sheer determination of the man, however, showed no signs of fading. He looked positively radiant when he joined the other members of Queen in the television studios as part of Cilla Black's *Goodbye To The Eighties*—this would be televised on New Year's Eve, when viewers would see the group receiving a *TV Times* award for Best Band of the Eighties. Then at the end of November, Queen flew to Montreux to begin work at the Mountain Stidios on their new album, while Freddie still had the strength to sing. It would be their last, and best. Mary Austin explained:

> It was the one thing that gave him much happiness. It made him feel alive inside, through the pain he was experiencing. I think that fed the light inside. Each morning there was something else he was working for—it wasn't just taking him to the grave. There was something else he could make happen, and he did.

On 18 February 1990, Queen were presented with an accolade for Outstanding Contribution To British Music at the British Phonographic Awards. While some recipients could not be bothered to collect their awards personally, all four members of the group turned up. Immediately after the ceremony at the Dominion Theatre, they eschewed the celebrity dinner to attend a more important celebration, the twentieth anniversary of Queen—though the current line-up had not been completed until the arrival of John Deacon in 1971, the other three had begun using the name one year earlier.

The group hired Groucho's—a name which appealed to them for obvious reasons—a small club in Soho which they packed with close friends and retainers past and present—just about everyone who had helped, befriended or worked with Queen over the last two decades. The 400 partygoers included Liza Minnelli, Rod Stewart, Michael Winner, Barry Humphries and George Michael. Lata Mangeshkar and Prince Edward were invited, but could not attend. Each guest was greeted by Gina Wildes and Simon Cotton, a Page Three Girl and Page Seven Hunk from the *Sun*, who added that special 'royal' touch by donning guardsmen's uniforms and executing a dapper little drill—before turning around and revealing that their bottoms were bare!

For much of the time, Freddie held court at a table at the back of the club. There was nothing unusual about this, though the press suggested that he was hiding from them, for obvious reasons. Towards the end of the evening a huge cake was wheeled in, decorated with a Monopoly board whose property squares were all Queen hits. The media, however, were only interested in reporting two aspects of the evening: Debbie Leng's £150,000 platinum necklace, given to her by Roger Taylor—and Freddie's appearance. When he was snapped by a *Sun* photographer leaving the club during the early hours of the morning, looking pale and gaunt and walking unsteadily, there was no hiding the fact that here was a very sick man. Even so, he laughed off any suggestion that he was unwell—indeed, what else could he do?—and told one reporter, 'Ill, my dear? I've never felt better!' Later, Joe Fanelli called the newspaper to explain, 'Freddie isn't poorly. He's lost a little weight, granted, but he needed to because he was getting chubby. He always looks anaemic when he's not wearing his stage make-up. And he *was* a little pissed, like everyone else.' Fanelli's comments were more or less ignored. The press had made up their own minds what to say about Freddie, right or wrong.

A few weeks later, Freddie returned to Montreux to resume work on the new album, which was to be called *Innuendo*. He told Peter Stein of *Top 40*, 'I'm pleased with my vocals on this album. *Innuendo* is a word I often use in Scrabble. For Queen it's a perfect title!' One of the first tracks to be completed was 'Delilah', Freddie's amusing homage to his favourite cat which contained the plum line, 'And then you make me mad when you pee all over my Chippendale suite.'

This was also a time of soothing, solitary walks along the shore of Lake Geneva, and visits to the quaint little building Freddie had nicknamed 'The Duck House', where he liked to sit in silent contemplation, watching the swans gliding back and forth on the water. Here he wrote a beautiful poem, an ode to the winter he would never see in this his most cherished spot on earth—the only place he could come to evade the media intrusion which was making his life a misery elsewhere. It would take several years, however, for 'A Winter's Tale' to emerge—hardly anyone knew it had been written and taped until several years after his death. Listening to it now sends shivers down the spine.

The *Innuendo* album, however, was taking longer to complete than had been anticipated, on account of Freddie's failing health. In June he was fitted with a tiny chest catheter so that his medication could be administered quickly and intravenously—in the studio itself, if necessary –ensuring as little delay as possible. Such was his strength of will that, while there was breath in his increasingly frail body, he was determined never to give in.

In July 1990, when work on *Innuendo* transferred to London's Metropolis Studios, the press became really troublesome as each morning a near-military-style operation was mounted to smuggle Freddie out of Garden Lodge without being seen. Such manoevres, naturally, only attracted more attention, particularly as one or other of his minders usually yelled some obscenity at the pack of photographers who tried to rush his limousine.

The ever-faithful Mary Austin later remembered this harrowing period, saying, 'Freddie was in tremendous pain, but he forced himself to continue. Working gave him the courage to face his illness.' The rest of the group and his entourage closed ranks around him, forming what they hoped would prove an impenetrable barrier from the press and scandalmongers. During the research for this book I was told that a journalist believed to have been Queen-friendly—paid by Queen Productions to keep a watchful eye on his colleagues—was actually earning more money feeding them information. Henceforth, Freddie would hardly have a waking moment's peace, and a few weeks later the poor man was dealt another savage blow—one of his most cherished friends, Joe Fanelli, told him that he too was dying of AIDS.

Even during these final months, Freddie put others before himself. Once he had recovered from the shock, so that Fanelli might have some independence when he was no longer around, Freddie bought him a place of his own. This was a small house in Chiswick, on the market for £160,000, and the estate agent was told to ensure that the owner was not at home when Freddie called to inspect it—though he was recognised by a neighbour. He paid up-front in cash and, as had happened with the Mews, the vendor was told in no uncertain terms to relocate as soon as possible.

It had to happen eventually, of course. Lee Brooks, a photographer with the *Sunday Mirror*, got close enough to Freddie to take a clear picture, and this appeared as an exclusive on 23 September. To be fair, in Brooks' photograph Freddie does not *look* ill—slimmer, perhaps, but certainly not ill. The giveaway the way in which the editorial said he had shuffled towards his car. There was more consternation, a few weeks later, when he failed to turn up at Cliff Richard's fiftieth birthday party, and such was the pressure on Queen by this time that Brian

May found himself compelled to inform the press, 'Freddie's okay, but he's been quite rough lately. He definitely hasn't got AIDS, but I think his wild rock 'n' roll lifestyle has caught up with him. A lot of the strain has been on him in dealing with the public. I think he just needs a break.'

The crunch came days later, when Freddie was snapped with his doctor-friend, Gordon Atkinson, leaving the latter's Harley Street surgery. Wearing a plain grey suit that looked several sizes too big for him, and bent forward, it was clearly an effort for him to cross the street to Atkinson's car. Jim Hutton had bought him a stick, which he had refused to use even at home, preferring brief work-outs on an exercise cycle. The pair then drove the 150 yards to Freddie's favourite eaterie, Albert Roux's Le Gavroche. And of course, less than an hour later the press swooped, forcing Freddie and Atkinson to effect an exit via the back door. The man sitting at the table next to Freddie told reporters, 'I never noticed anything. And who *is* this Freddie Mercury, anyhow?' Five minutes and a few hundred pounds later, his story had been amended for the benefit of the tabloids: 'I recognized Freddie at once. He was quite chatty and cheerful, but he looked *awful*.'

The photographer responsible this this and other heartbreaking pictures was 23-year-old Jason Fraser, described by the *News of the World* as 'one of a shadowy group of highly-paid, deadly professionals who scour the streets in search of the perfect shots.' To which the aforementioned friend who had first discovered Freddie's Karposi's Sarcoma responded, 'They said that, but if they'd have got there first, they wouldn't have hesitated to publish a photograph of Freddie themselves. The tabloids were *all* the same. It was just a question of which one would be first to hit the jackpot.' For almost a month, Fraser had been liaising with contacts, acquiring details of his quarry's every movement outside Garden Lodge—though Freddie was by now a virtual recluse, enjoying only the company of his closest friends, and his beloved cats, emerging now and then to visit Mary Austin and her son, Richard, who had been born in February. During the afternoon of the shoot Fraser had lain in wait, watching Gordon Atkinson's surgery from an upstairs window. He had trailed Freddie and the doctor to Le Gavroche, taking innumerable pictures with the camera concealed under his armpit. More candid shots were taken as the pair were leaving.

The photographs presented Fraser with a moral dilemma, he claimed, for two weeks deliberating over what to do with them: destroy them, file them for future use—or take the money and expose Freddie's anguish to the world. He opted for the latter, earning himself paparazzi notoriety, and many enemies within the Queen camp. Some years later, when it was too late to make amends, Fraser explained that he had only sold the picture—for an alleged five-figure sum—because he hoped that in publishing it he might change the public's perception of AIDS, that as someone famous was dying from the disease—as had happened with Rock Hudson—much of the homophobia might stop. He told the *News of the World Magazine* in 1995:

> There was this guy, adored by millions, who had been struck down by a terrible disease that you could get no matter how famous or rich you were. But he was there, in the street—anyone could have seen him. There's no way I would have broken into a hospital or climbed his garden wall to get my pictures. I saw him, and I admired him. No one, no matter what their sexual preferences might be, deserved what Freddie Mercury got.

To a certain extent, Fraser was right in his opinion, though this did not excuse the way he had acquired his pictures. There was considerable sympathy from the general public over Freddie's plight, and that of his fellow sufferers. The attitude of the media, on the other hand, was unforgivably ruthless. 'Fraser didn't have any morals at all,' said Jacky Gunn of the Queen Fan Club. 'He was *only* interested in the money. I only hope it did him some good. What he did certainly made Freddie's life a misery.' And Holly Johnson, the Frankie Goes To Hollywood frontman who announced not long afterwards that he too was HIV positive, hit out, 'Seeing pictures of Freddie Mercury on the cover of the papers, looking emaciated, that was really *vile*.'

For Queen, meanwhile, it was business as usual. Freddie bravely refused, while he possessed the strength, to allow his illness to interfere with the group's future plans, even though he might not be there to reap the benefits of what was being sown right now. Dissatisfied with their American record company, Capitol, whom they held partly responsible for their slump in popularity in the United States, the group had instructed Jim Beach to 'sort out a deal'—not an easy task for an act who had not had a major hit in the country for six years. The bargaining factor, however, came when Beach purchased from Capitol the rights to Queen's back catalogue. This meant that whoever signed them would be permitted to release their *entire* output on digitally re-mastered compact discs for the first time—effectively improving the sound quality of their music, even moreso than the British re-mastering on CD by EMI—and earn everyone involved with Queen a fortune.

In November 1990, a $10 million deal was finalized with Hollywood Records, a fledgling label started earlier in the year by the multi-million-dollar Walt Disney Corporation. Peter Patermo, the company's president and a huge Queen fan, predicted that their next album would be their biggest ever, and told a press conference, 'Queen are a greatly undervalued asset. It's a great catalogue. I paid a lot of money for it—a Queen's ransom, to be precise—and before too long they're going to be ruling the charts!' There was another sweetener which Hollywood

Records could not fail to take into consideration. Freddie Mercury, the very soul and essence of Queen, was dying, and everyone knew since the deaths of Jim Morrisson and Jimi Hendrix that most rock legends earned more dead than alive—a sad but unalterable fact which had been proved far too often.

Amazingly, bearing in mind that most of the newspapers had already drafted Freddie's obituary, it was one of the publications that he despised the most, *Today*, which came up with a suitable defence on 14 January 1991, the day that the 'Innuendo' single was released. The first of a two-part series, 'Freddie Mercury: The Magic & The Mystique', bore the subtitle, 'Crazy Little Thing Called Love Made Me Change My Life', and purported to explain how Freddie had amended his lifestyle since cradling Mary Austin's son in his arms, on the steps of the church on the day of his christening. Most of the editorial was hogwash, of course—Freddie had never spoken to the newspaper—though the journalist, Richard Middleton, could only be commended for attempting to wean his colleagues away from some of the lurid stories which had circulated since the publication of the Jason Fraser photograph.

According to Middleton, Freddie had given up his daily bottle of vodka, his large intake of rich Indian food, his Rolls-Royce and his voracious sexual appetite—all true—also that he had enrolled with a gym for regular workouts, causing his weight to drop from 170 to 125 pounds, which was not true at all. Freddie's choice of sexuality—itself entirely normal—was also defended by his friend, Jacky Gunn, who concluded, 'Freddie's a permanent bachelor. He has tried and failed in heterosexual relationships and now realizes that he simply doesn't need to. He jokes that he'd much rather have another cat!'

Few of Freddie's detractors, of course, took the *Today* article seriously—they had made up their minds to persecute him, and nothing would ever change their hostile, homophobic and bigoted opinions. It was Paul Prenter, who had neither seen nor spoken to Freddie since being ousted from his circle, who shopped him to the press in an act of pure spite. Fearing there could be reprisals, should he ever speak to British reporters, Prenter called the *New York Globe* at the end of January and offered a statement:

> Freddie is just a shadow. His body is frail and stooped and he shuffles along like an old man. He used to be bouncy and vibrant, but now he looks desperately sick. He's lost an alarming amount of weight and his clothes hang on him. No matter what they say officially, he's suffering from something far worse than the flu. I am desperately afraid that it might be AIDS. Freddie has led a very wild life.

Prenter's revelations were printed alongside the Jason Fraser photograph, headed, 'AIDS Ravages Rocker Queen'. Ironically, within a few months, Prenter would himself succumb to the disease. To a certain extent, Freddie took much of his frustration out on friends. Peter Straker and Barbara Valentin were among the first to fall by the wayside, as David Evans explained:

> There's a condition called AIDS-anger, where those who are terminally ill get terribly angry for no reason. It's an anger which goes with the fact that these people are alive, and you're going to die. Barbara and Straker fell under that particular shadow because they were unable to handle his anger. Freddie cut out a lot of people at the end of his life, especially the ones who had lived with him through his hectic, wild years. He couldn't cope with the people who only adored him as that boisterous, partying, devil-may-care person. He was in incredible pain for the final twelve months of his life yet he still had

to try and keep going. So, he gathered about him only the people he knew would sustain his soul, the ones he could keep up with in terms of the old days.

'Innuendo', the single, entered the British charts at Number 1—the first time Queen had occupied the top slot since 'Under Pressure' in 1981. In America, Hollywood Records, aware that radio stations would be reluctant to air a record running in excess of six minutes, released 'Headlong' instead—a wise choice, for it peaked at Number 3. *Innuendo,* the album, came out three weeks later—again it went straight to Number 1, selling 250,000 copies in its first week alone, annoying the British music press, who had unanimously reviled it.

In America, the album was released on 5 February in a fanfare of publicity. The $400,000 launch took place aboard the *Queen Mary*, the 81,000-ton Cunard-White Star liner which had recently been purchased by the Walt Disney Corporation and turned into a hotel. Permanently moored in concrete, it stood next to Howard Hughes' famous plane, *Spruce Goose*, in Long Beach, California. The 1700 guests marvelled at the Queen performance staged by illuminated robots, which proved so popular that it had to be repeated, and the evening was rounded off with one of the most impressive firework displays California had ever seen when $100,000 worth of them were let off to the strains of 'Bohemian Rhapsody'. But whereas Brian May and Roger Taylor turned up for the party, John Deacon did not—one source citing 'family reasons', the other saying parties were no longer his scene. This infuriated the executives at Hollywood Records, one of whom hit out, 'This company has invested $10 million in these four—they should *all* be here, family or no family.' Though *Innuendo* only reached Number 30 on the *Billboard* album chart, Hollywood Records were far from disappointed. After six years in a virtual rock wilderness, Queen were back.

The covers for the album and the four singles taken from it contained a series of pencil drawings by the early-19th century illustrator, Grandville, hand-coloured and only slightly amended by Richard Gray. The one used for the album was entitled 'A Juggler Of Universes', and depicted a shock-haired clown doing just that—the addition of a banana was Freddie's idea. Simon Fowler, a well-known rock photographer, was commissioned for the group's publicity shots, though of the hundred or so pictures taken by him, only three were seen by fans because the remainder were deemed 'unsuitable' by Queen Productions. One of the group looking somewhat elongated, and another of them lying horizontally on individual shelves—thus arranged, it is thought, so that Freddie's by now drastic weight loss might not be so readily discernible. The third shot depicted him sitting unusually apart from the other three. The media speculation that he had been touched up to make him appear healthier was hotly refuted by Queen's publicist and agent, Roxy Meade, who only added to the confusion and intrigue by saying of the photographs, 'The problem is the technique used, where only half of them are in focus at any one time,' and of the group's imminent plans, 'There's no chance of them doing interviews or going on TV. I'm waiting for the video to be finished.'

Grandville's drawings also formed the basis for the £120,000 *Innuendo* video, brought to life on the screen by the animator Jerry Hibbert, winning him an American 'Gold Camera' award. A six-and-a-half-minute Grand Guignol masque, it also featured a fandango with plasticine figures, animated sketches of the group, and film clips of the Nuremberg Rally, the funeral of Freddie's former singing idol Oum Kalthoum, and battle footage from World War II—the latter replaced at the last moment by fragments of Hungarian folk-dancing when, unexpectedly, war broke out in the Gulf.

In America, Hollywood capitalized on the Gulf War, issuing a limited edition CD to the troops—President Bush's victory speech, superimposed over Queen's 'We Are The Champions'. This was allegedly to compensate for the BBC's so-called 'War & Peace' list which recommended that songs such as 'Another One Bites The Dust'—for obvious reasons extremely popular in the Gulf—Lulu's Eurovision winner, 'Boom-Bang-A-Bang', and Cher's 'Bang-Bang' should not be played for the duration of the conflict.

The fact that the *Innuendo* video did not contain footage of Queen themselves only supplemented the rumours that Freddie was too ill to be seen by his fans. For this reason he insisted on making a personal appearance in the video for the next single, 'I'm Going Slightly Mad', which was filmed by the Torpedo Twins at London's Limehouse Studios in mid-February. Needless to say, the media awaited the outcome with bated breath.

This song, a low-key affair but an absolute corker all the same, was rich with Freddie's camp, puckish humour—a Colonial trait described by Roger Taylor as 'Noel Coward meets Oscar Wilde meets Led Zeppelin', and the amusing, largely monochrome video suited this perfectly. The entire £200,000 escapade was engineered by Freddie himself. Stopping every few minutes to issue instructions to his team and to rest, he wore a £900 shaggy wig and lots of pancake make-up to impersonate Lord Byron, produced classic lines such as, 'I think I'm a banana tree!', and cavorted with live penguins and a man in a gorilla suit—while John Deacon gurned in a joker's hat and played with a yo-yo, Roger Taylor wore a steaming kettle on his head and rode a tricycle, and Brian May dressed as a penguin with a large yellow beak and silver fingernails. Freddie then traded his poet's garb for a stunning blue and yellow swansdown and ostrich-feather redincote. A masterpiece!

The video shoot suffered a "drama" when one of the penguins—Cleo, who Freddie had taken to and fussed over like a baby, mindless of his agony—urinated on the sumptuous leather sofa, missing him by inches. 'The Day a P-P-P-Penguin Decided To Go For A P-P-P-Pee,' ran the headline in the *People*, harking back to the famous television commercials for the chocolate biscuit of the same name. Freddie told Kate Molloy, 'I wanted to make this video as memorable as possible. I've always wanted to co-star in a video with a gorilla and a group of penguins. A little bit of Queen madness is wanted right now, so don't bother to question our sanity!'

The press were unconvinced that Freddie was not ill. At the end of April, he was reported to be receiving round-the-clock medical care, virtually bedridden, and losing his sight. Even so, such was his strength of will that by early May he and the rest of Queen were beavering away at the Mountain Studios on their next album. It would be here, towards the end of August, that Freddie would record his final song, 'Mother Love', a beautiful pastiche which contained his final, tragic credo:

I long for peace before I die....

But had this troubled, persecuted young man found such a thing in this once-unloved haven, far from the prying eyes of an increasingly menacing media? Brian May believed he had, telling a radio interviewer not long afterwards, 'He tried for the high notes, paused, downed a couple of vodkas, and got it right. He could hardly stand on account of his pain, yet I never once saw him put his head in his hands and say he'd had enough.' And Roger Taylor said in the same interview, 'The last thing he wanted was to draw attention to any kind of weakness or frailty. He didn't want any kind of pity.'

Freddie had recently purchased a sumptuous three-bedroomed penthouse in Montreux, with panoramic views of the lake and city, and he had hired the best—and costliest—interior designers in Switzerland to make the place 'homely', tragically for no other reason than spending for spending's sake, for he had already decided that he had had enough. Wishing to end the struggle—according to Jim Hutton, who now broke the news that he too was HIV positive—Freddie had decided to stop taking his medication. Yet in England, Brian May's secretary was following instructions and telling the press, 'Freddie is absolutely fine. He has been going to auctions every day for the last week.'

Just ten weeks after 'I'm Going Slightly Mad', Queen released another single, 'Headlong', which many fans found considerably less appealing than the B-side of the CD single, 'Mad The Swine'. Freddie had written this twenty years earlier for one of Queen's albums: it had been recorded in 1972, but never used until now.

On 30 May, Freddie, Roger Taylor and John Deacon spent most of the day in the studio with Rudi Dolezal, shooting the video for their next American single, 'These Are The Days Of Our Lives'. Brian May was still promoting *Innuendo* in the United States and would film his contribution a little later. The video was to complement a television documentary, *Days Of Our Lives*, charting the Queen story for their new generation of fans. Freddie was distressed to learn that its narrator was Axl Rose, of the heavy rock group, Guns 'N' Roses. Over the past few years, Rose had issued a number of extremely unpleasant anti-gay, racist statements to the media—one of Freddie's long-standing ambitions had been to meet him, and spit in his eye.

The 'These Are The Days Of Our Lives' video was Freddie's saying goodbye to his fans, his very last piece of film, one which ends with the half-whispered, heartfelt words, 'I still love you!'

In Britain, Queen's next single was 'The Show Must Go On', without any doubt the most moving, portentous song Freddie ever performed. *Everything* about it pointed towards that final, now unstoppable curtain. 'My make-up may be flaking, but my smile stays on,' he defiantly opines, before committing himself to

188

the inevitable, 'I'll face it with a grin, I'm never giving in.' Few men could have faced up to their fate with such self-parodying courage. *This* is what made Freddie Mercury so very special to so many people. Many years later, the French singer Gregory Lemarchal (1983-2007) adopted it as his signature. The winner of the country's *Star Academy*, he became an overnight sensation, only to die of cystic fibrosis, aged just twenty-three, plunging France into profound mourning. Queen's single, the last to be issued in Freddie's lifetime, was released on 14 October. It was followed, two weeks later, by their second compilation album, *Greatest Hits II*, which gave them their eighth Number One and which was complimented with a *Greatest Flix II* video.

When Freddie returned to Garden Lodge early in September 1991 after visiting his Swiss apartment, he had to be secreted into the grounds via the entrance to the Mews, in the back of a friend's car. That same day he received a home visit from Dr Brian Gizzard, the head of the AIDS unit at London's Westminster Hospital. The press, having been tipped off that it was only a matter of time, refused to let him be. Sometimes there would be as many as seventy reporters and photographers hanging around the perimeter of the building, like vultures. Some climbed the walls or perched their tripods on ladders, training their lenses on the upstairs windows for the slightest movement.

Towards the end of the month, Montserrat Caballé, who since Freddie had told her of his illness had called him at least once a week, now rang to say that she was coming to London for a recording session. Freddie begged her not to put herself through the ordeal of coming to the house. She told me:

> I was in London to record the aria 'Christine' from Phantom of the Opera. I was doing it for him because he loved it, so I rang him from the studio and played it down the phone. He was both happy and sad. Happy that

I'd done this just for him, sad that we would never see each other again, and as I put the phone down, I said to myself, 'What a brave, wonderful man this is.'

Friends and loved ones who did visit Garden Lodge were jostled and interrogated, particularly Mary Austin and Dave Clark who, with Jim Hutton, Joe Fanelli and Peter Freestone took it in turns to sit at Freddie's bedside. On one occasion Hutton threatened to thump an aggressive reporter. On another, Roger Taylor was blinded by popping flashbulbs and drove his car into the back of one of the ever-present police cars. The tension also deepened the rift which had apparently been developing for some time between Mary and Hutton—particularly when, according to the latter, Mary had suggested that Freddie should remove his wedding ring because she felt it might cause him discomfort if his fingers began swelling, as he approached the end. For Hutton, who spent more time with Freddie than anyone during these final days, this was a trip to Calvary, as he recalled, 'I often used to cry on my own, but I made sure Freddie never saw me upset. Throughout the day, for him I'd be strong, but his dying face haunted my nights, and I'd always end up crying myself to sleep.'

At Midnight, on 23 November, Freddie himself ended all the speculation by issuing a statement—though some believe that he was so ill by now, it may have been prepared earlier, ready for when the time came—which stunned not just his millions of fans, but those friends outside his very intimate circle:

Following the enormous conjecture in the press over the last two weeks, I wish to confirm that I have tested HIV positive and have AIDS. I felt it correct to keep this information private in order to protect the privacy of those around me. However, the time has come for my friends and fans around the world to know the truth, and

190

I hope that everyone will join me in the fight against this terrible disease.

The sad news made the front pages of just about every national newspaper in the world—even in Russia and China, where Queen had never performed. Yet even as Freddie's fans were choking back the tears and trying to take this in, news flashes were pronouncing even grimmer tidings. At 7.01 p.m. on Sunday 24 November 1991, the greatest rock star and showman of his generation had passed away.

Freddie was just forty-five years old, and only weeks before, in his last known interview, he had told his friend David Wigg of the *Daily Express*:

> I don't really think about when I'm dead, or how they are going to remember me. I don't really think about it. It's up to them. When I'm dead, who cares? I don't!'

"I still love you!"

Ten: Love Conquers All

It is not the purpose of this book to enlarge on Freddie Mercury's final, agonizing hours. These were recorded three years after his death by Jim Hutton in clinical, distressing—and some of the singer's close friends have alleged—greatly exaggerated detail. One of these, who requested to me identified only as "M", demanded that the record be set straight:

> That part of the story, where he was with Freddie, is very inaccurate. Jimmy wasn't even in the room, and all that about Freddie's leg breaking is nonsense. Peter Freestone was in the house, but he wasn't in the room either. The only person with Freddie when he died was Dave Clark, and he phoned me as soon as it happened. All the other stories are lies.

Though Freddie had been critically ill, the end came sooner than anyone had anticipated. Dave Clark, who has not spoken publicly since, was the first to submit to a press interview. Fighting back the tears, he said, 'For me he was a rare gem, a rare painting. He was a rare person, but he suffered and when he slipped away, I knew he was going to a better place.' Mary Austin, who had spent the day at Garden Lodge—leaving ten minutes before Freddie died, promising that she would be back the next morning—had the task of informing the Bulsaras. She said:

> He faced his illness with incredible bravery, but he did suffer, mentally and emotionally, as well as physically. His mother saw him eight days before he died, but he became very ill very quickly, and he really didn't want them [his parents] to see him.

Queen's publicist, Roxy Meade, issued a brief statement to the effect that Freddie had died of bronchial pneumonia, brought on by AIDS. Brian May, speaking on breakfast television, also praised his friend's courage, and defended Freddie's decision not to tell the world the truth concerning his illness: 'It would have been very easy to put on his death certificate just "pneumonia", and it could have side-stepped everything. But he said, "I have got this and there is no shame, no stigma."'

The remaining members of Queen issued their own statement:

> We feel overwhelming grief that he is gone, sadness that he should be cut down at the height of his creativity, but above all great pride in the courageous way that he lived and died. It has been a privilege for us to have shared such magical times.

Brian May also composed a moving letter, which he published in the fan club's Christmas magazine, thanking Freddie's admirers for their love and support—an affection which would not simply flourish, but escalate. Two years later, Mary Austin conveyed her own message to the fans in the same magazine:

> With the terrible stigma associated with AIDS, you [the fans] have shone through. You didn't turn away, you saw the man beyond the disease, loved him through it, despite and beyond it....By your continued loyalty to Freddie you help lift the spirit of others, also affected.

Montserrat Caballé sobbed unashamedly at a press conference in Barcelona:

I'm beside myself with grief. I loved Freddie as a friend and I respected him as a musician and a composer. I knew he was dying, and I bitterly hoped he would be cured. Freddie was a very tough person. He always used to tell me that he had to make his own way in life, carrying his own luggage....There is one line in that song [the aria 'Christine', from Phantom of the Opera]—'I hope you are here is some way another time'—which will always remind me of my lovely Freddie.

Kenny Everett—who himself would die of an AIDS-related illness in April 1995, aged fifty—offered a typically zany tribute, but heartfelt tribute: 'He was a genius. But I won't be going to his funeral. After all, Freddie won't be there!' Another back-handed compliment came from James 'Trip' Khalaf, the soundman on Queen's tours between 1976 and 1986, who said, 'Freddie had no marketable skills, so what else could he have been but a huge, bombastic rock star? And the son-of-a-bitch did a great job!'

The backlash began at once, as hundreds of fans queued up outside Garden Lodge to pay their last respects—not in the conventional sense as with other legends, being allowed into the domicile to file past the catafalque, but simply by being there, while radio stations around the globe were playing Freddie's records virtually non-stop. The broadsheets proffered respectable eulogies, though the tabloids would only afford Freddie's musical skills second place after his sexual exploits in what must certainly be some of the most poisonous pieces of journalism since their attacks on Rock Hudson, six years earlier. A typical article would begin, 'This is not a moral judgement....' before launching into a tirade of insults which in most cases was totally unnecessary and often hypocritical. None is worth repeating in this book.

Initially Freddie was championed by Virginia Bottomley, the Minister of Health, who applauded him for the bravery of his announcement, adding that this would now 'encourage others to recognize the dangers of the disease and practise prevention.' Dr Patrick Dixon, the founder of the charity AIDS Care Education & Training, spoke out in his defence, saying, 'His behaviour *did* change, but not in time to prevent his own death. The media should now concentrate on helping to prevent *more* HIV infection, not on harassing people who are vulnerable.'

His staunchest defence came from Terry Sanderson, in his powerful 'Mediawatch' column in *Gay Times*, whose blistering condemnation of the tabloids began with a borrowed phrase from veteran journalist Woodrow Wyatt: 'We're badly served by our broadcasting and press commentators. Most are too stupid or too lazy to examine the facts behind the issues.' Admitting how Freddie had caused problems for himself by not issuing his statement until too late, Terry explained why some the press had singled out Freddie in particular for their hate campaign:

> AIDS hysteria was past its peak, but it was still powerful enough for the press to need a focus, and Freddie provided it. From the tabloids' point of view, he died just at the right moment. He was perceived by them as a standard homosexual—promiscuous and uncaring about health and safety. That's how uneductated many of them were and still are.

Jim Hutton always maintained that Freddie had never wanted to make a statement, that *he* as Freddie's 'next of kin' had only allowed Jim Beach to persuade him to release it so as to prevent the tabloids from acquiring another scoop. He wrote in his book, *Mercury & Me*, 'It was Freddie's way of saying to those so eagerly awaiting his death, "Fuck you!!' Others have said that he

196

was too ill be aware of his surroundings, let alone sufficiently coherent to dictate any statement—that, had he wanted the world to know the precise details of his illness, he would have spoken out some time before, as Rock Hudson had done, and attracted considerably more media sympathy. In fact, by having *his* illness revealed by a hospital spokeswoman three months before his death, Rock had made matters infinitely worse. Effectively, Freddie—or whoever was responsible for that statement—had done the right thing.

David Evans shared the same theory as many of Freddie's friends: 'Freddie couldn't *afford* to make anything public, not for selfish reasons but for Queen's sake and for the sake of their wives, children and employees. He was terrified of what the public's reaction would have been towards *them*.' And Mary Austin added, defensively, 'It took him a long, long time to accept for himself that he had AIDS, so how could he tell the world when he couldn't accept it for himself?'

Freddie's funeral, during the afternoon of 27 November 1991 at West London's Kensal Green Crematorium, was a subdued, dignified and essentially private affair, attended by thirty or so close friends and fourteen members of his family—most of whom had not seen him for years. The family-only ceremony preceding it earlier in the day had been conducted entirely in the Zoroastrian faith. His parents, among the handful of mourners there not wearing black, had insisted on this. The chanting by two white-robed priests, calling for the soul of the departed to be transported to *qaroghman bahest*, or eternal heaven, was almost entirely in Avasta, an ancient language of the Parsees. Only the words 'sit' and 'stand' were pronounced in English.

Mary Austin was escorted into the chapel by Dave Clark, who had travelled with her in the first car, replacing Jim Hutton at the last moment. Hutton, Peter Freestone and Joe Fanelli were relegated to the third car, behind Jim Beach. 'The three of us felt let down,' Hutton later said, claiming that Mary had deliberately snubbed him by failing to recognize his next-of-kin status. 'We'd been the ones with Freddie through thick and thin during his illness. It seemed no sooner that he was dead than we were being pushed aside.' Many would have agreed, of course, that Freddie had loved this woman more than anyone—even more than he had loved his parents. Within the chapel, however, Clark moved to another pew so that these three could sit with Mary at the front.

Mary's wreath was inscribed, 'For my dearest with my deepest love, from your old faithful.' Brian May's and Anita Dobson's read, 'Dear Freddie, we will love you forever,' while Roger Taylor's bore a simple, 'Goodbye old friend, peace at last.' Jim Hutton sent a swan made of white flowers, with a lengthy poetic message which concluded, 'You died as you lived—everyone's friend.' Elton John, who wept unconsolably throughout the twenty-minute service, sent a heart of one-hundred salmon roses which he had inscribed, 'Thank you for being my friend.' In all there were over 400 floral tributes from around the world, conveyed to Kensal Green by five Daimlers. These were later donated to AIDS hospices.

Freddie's oak coffin, adorned with a single red rose, was transported from the Rolls-Royce hearse into the chapel to the strains of Aretha Franklin's 'Precious Lord Take My Hand'. A little later, Montserrat Caballé's recording of Verdi's 'D'amor sull-alli rose' from *Il Trovatore*, was relayed through loudspeakers. These were arguably the only sections of the ceremony Freddie would have approved of, for he had long since rejected his faith.

There was also a moment which would have amused him, as a cat lover, when a large black tom unceremoniously nudged its way through the cortege.

It was over.

Epilogue: Never To Be Forgotten

With *Greatest Hits II* still clinging to the top of the album charts, *Bohemian Rhapsody* was re-released as a double A-side with 'These Are The Days Of Our Lives' on 9 December 1991. Precisely fifteen years after it had first topped the charts, it did so again, remaining at the top for five weeks. Most importantly, it earned over £1 million in royalties which were donated to the Terrence Higgins Trust. Brian May and Roger Taylor presented the cheque to the organization in April 1992, at the Ivor Novello Awards, where Freddie also won a posthumous award for the best-selling A-side of 1991, and May an award for best television commercial theme for 'Driven By You', written for Ford Cars. The first single from his début album, *Back To The Light*, had been released the day after Freddie's death. The most successful solo project thus far in May's career, the single reached Number 6 in the charts. Roger Taylor told the audience, 'The best way to fight this appalling illness is to make sure everybody knows about AIDS and *how* it can be fought. Freddie's best-known song has helped do that.'

In America, the re-released 'Bohemian Rhapsody' reached Number 2 in the charts, with the proceeds going to the Magic Johnson AIDS Foundation—something Freddie may not have approved of, according to 'out' tennis champion Martina Navratilova, who launched an attack on the baseball player who had recently declared himself HIV positive, attracting a huge amount of the public sympathy denied Freddie—because Johnson stressed he had caught the virus after sleeping with hundreds of *women*.

What promised to be the ultimate tribute, *A Concert For Life: The Freddie Mercury Concert For AIDS Awareness*, took place at Wembley on Easter Monday, 20 April 1992 with the surviving members of Queen joining what the promoters promised would be 'a host of stars' on the hugest stage the venue had seen since Queen's last concerts in the summer of 1986.

The tabloids questioned the theme of the proposed show, with the *Daily Mail*'s Toby Young leading the attack: 'AIDS *awareness*. That was a little odd considering Freddie Mercury didn't make the world aware that he was suffering from AIDS until twelve hours before he died of it.' Even so, all 72,000 tickets for the event sold out in just four hours, before the final guest list was announced—such was the hype that many forecast another *Live Aid.*

Unfortunately, much of the concert comprised barely second-rate entertainment unworthy of an artist of Freddie's calibre. Elaine Paige had not been invited to give the event a touch of class, nor had representatives from pop's camp element much loved by Freddie, such as Boy George or Erasure, to make it sparkle. Montserrat Caballé *had* been asked to appear, but her punishing work schedule would not accommodate an extra engagement. 'I was in Seville for Expo '92,' she told me, 'And I asked if I could take part via satellite. Unfortunately, they couldn't make the connection. I was very upset because I was singing in "La Galliarda", an opera which Freddie had loved. Still, I *was* with him in spirit.'

The comparative amateurism of the concert and its participants was inadvertently highlighted by the producers of the live televised event when they played video and film clips of the real thing between acts: Freddie Mercury, proving ultimately that he had possessed qualities they had only dreamed of, namely showmanship and charisma. The concert did not bring in any inordinate amount of money for its intended charity on the actual day, certainly not in relation to its size. Of the £2 million grossed in ticket sales, over half of this was deducted for 'production costs' and expenses. However, with rental sales to worldwide television companies—it reached an estimated audience of 1.2 billion—and the sales of records and DVDs, it eventually raised over £20 million.

The Boston-based ensemble, Extreme, excelled with their Queen rock-medley, but their tuneless rendition of 'Love Of My Life', the song Freddie had once dubbed his 'Hymne a l'amour', left a great deal to be desired. Def Leppard, Guns 'N' Roses, Metallica, Paul Young and Roger Daltrey succeeded only in making a lot of noise and completely failed to resurrect any of the magic associated with Freddie. Toby Young, again writing for the *Daily Mail*, denounced Annie Lennox's spot as 'a masterpiece of stupidity', and her duet of 'Under Pressure' with David Bowie as 'tawdry'. For once he was probably being *too* kind. Bowie himself was criticised for his boastful comment, referring to his hedonistic days on the same tour-circuit as Queen, 'We all used to play the same dance-halls and theatres....we slept with a lot of the same people, too.' Bowie was further brought to task by A N Wilson of the *Daily Telegraph*—for sinking to his knees and reciting an unconvincing if not ludicrous Lord's Prayer.

The shock item on the bill had to be Guns 'N' Roses, a group which Freddie had loathed. In 1988, one of their songs contained the deeply unpleasant line, 'Immigrants and faggots spread disease'—a line which Freddie believed had been directed at him personally—since which time their concerts had been heckled by gay rights activists. Their frontman, Axl Rose, received so many threats before the Wembley show that it was rumoured he would pull out of the proceedings, particularly when he failed to turn up for rehearsals. Now, as he took to the stage, he received the vitriol he deserved from Freddie's many gay fans, and *Gay Times'* Richard Smith, curiously writing in the present tense, observed:

201

When they play, a threatened protest is inaudible above the deafening cheers. Elton John puts his arm around Axl Rose, a gesture caused perhaps less by an uncontrollable groundswell of affection than that this is what one does at such events. Whatever, Axl looks extremely uncomfortable. It's unlikely that he's the only person in that stadium who loved Freddie but hated faggots.

Lisa Stansfield and George Michael on the other hand were sheer perfection—she 'vacuuming' the stage with 'I Want To Break Free', he with 'Somebody To Love', and together with an absolutely sublime 'These Are The Days Of Our Lives'.

George Michael was so good, in fact, that rumours soon began circulating that he would become Queen's new frontman, a role which he never would have dreamed of accepting, and one which in any case would not have been tolerated by Freddie's admirers. 'That concert was the proudest moment of my career. I was living out my childhood fantasy,' he reflected afterwards, proudly sporting the silver and red rhinestones AIDS symbol presented to him by Elizabeth Taylor. Elton John too offered a powerhouse performance—one Freddie would have been proud of—with 'The Show Must Go On'. Liza Minnelli, on the other hand, along with the band and a full cast, struggled through the most lamentable 'We Are The Champions' one could possibly imagine—before Freddie himself in all his regal, ceremonial glory rounded off the event on the big screen, while the stadium erupted into an exuberant 'God Save The Queen'.

The heroes of the evening, however, were the trio of May, Deacon and Taylor—and Elizabeth Taylor, to whom this book is dedicated. 'Freddie was denied the privilege of growing old,' Brian May said. 'But in forty-five years he packed in enough living for a dozen lifetimes.' Accompanying himself on the piano he then sang a tremulous 'Too Much Love Will Kill You'—with such intense emotion that one can only wonder at how much sadness one man may shoulder without breaking down. There were no exceptions—he absolutely swept away every other act on the bill.

Elizabeth Taylor, despite being heckled by a group of Guns 'N' Roses fans—'I'll *get off* in a minute. I have something to say!'—was also clearly on the verge of tears. The undisputed champion of the gay man, gay rights and AIDS awareness, for nearly half a century she had offered solace to the troubled psyches of Montgomery Clift, James Dean, Richard Burton—and Rock Hudson, who she had helped through the final weeks of his illness, and even arranged his funeral. She had also raised over £10 million for AIDS charities in that one month alone after Freddie's death (at the time of her death in 2011, she would have raised a staggering $300 million for her own AIDS charities) and in a lengthy unscripted speech, Saint Elizabeth, as she had now become, urged the world to practise safe sex and syringe-sensibility. She concluded:

> We are here to celebrate the life of Freddie Mercury, an extraordinary rock star who rushed across our cultural landscape like a comet shooting across the sky. We are also here to tell the whole world that he, like others we have lost to AIDS, died before his time. The bright light of his talent still exhilarates us, even now that his life has been so cruelly extinguished. It needn't have happened. It shouldn't have happened. Please, let's not let it happen again.

The opera world paid its own, perhaps more stylish tribute to Freddie on 28 June, in a gala at the Banqueting House in London's Whitehall. It was organized and stage-managed by Peter Freestone, the man who had taught Freddie most of what he knew about the medium, and it comprised a performance of his favourite opera, *Il Trovatore*. Montserrat Caballé, the patron of the English Chamber Opera Touring Company which performed it, announced to the press, 'This gala is a fitting tribute by the opera community to a great composer and performed who is an immense loss to all spheres of music. I miss him very much.'

The proceeds from this concert were donated to the Mercury Phoenix Trust, the organization founded in Freddie's honour with the profits from the Wembley tribute—not just from ticket sales but from broadcasting, record and video rights. The trustees were Brian May, Roger Taylor, Mary Austin and Jim Beach. John Deacon refused his trusteeship—indeed, he had taken a lot of persuading to appear in the Wembley show, and has since played a minor role in other homages to Freddie because, it is alleged, he disapproves of the hype involved and prefers to remember his friend in his own way.

Freddie did not leave as much money as most people expected. In his last will, sealed just seven days before his death, and with Jim Beach and John Libson (his accountant) as executors, he left gross assets amounting to just over £8 million. A large portion of his wealth had been spent on medical care, largely at the Westminster Hospital, during the last years of his life. He had also bought Jim Hutton a house in Ireland, and anonymously donated £500,000 to AIDS research.

The main beneficiary, not surprisingly, was the loyal Mary Austin, who received half of his estate, plus whatever share of Queen's publishing and recording royalties would have gone to Freddie over the next fifty years, plus Garden Lodge and the Mews which alone were valued at £4 million. A further 25 per cent went to Freddie's sister, Kashmira Cooke, and the remaining 25 per cent was bequeathed to his parents—something of a surprise, for inasmuch as they had denounced his sexuality, they had always rejected his generosity, and in an earlier will had been left nothing. Though Freddie's mother always spoke warmly of her son, Bomi Bulsara went to his grave in 2003, still bearing a grudge against his son for never having given him grandchildren.

Jim Hutton, Joe Fanelli and Peter Freestone were each bequeathed £500,000, and Freddie left £100,000 to his chauffeur, Terry Giddings. There were, again surprisingly, no other legatees, and nothing was left to charity. In his lifetime Freddie had given millions to needy causes, but in death he was concerned only in providing for his loved ones.

It had been Freddie's wish that the trio of Hutton, Freestone and Fanelli remain at Garden Lodge for as long as they desired. One was dying, another soon would be. Unfortunately, this particular instruction had not been set down in writing, and just one week after Freddie's funeral, Mary Austin gave them twelve weeks' notice to leave her property. Not only this—while finding alternative accommodation, all three were compelled to move into the Mews while the Garden Lodge security system was reviewed and guards posted on duty, twenty-four hours a day.

Mary told David Wigg at the time of the men's eviction:

> It was always going to be awkward, and it would have been impossible for Jimmy to stay. Jimmy's relationship with Freddie was not one I could totally appreciate, so it left me at an advantage. He was let down by a lot of boyfriends. He'd become a star and people went for the trappings rather than looking at the heart. And Freddie had an enormous heart.

Joe Fanelli returned to America, where he died the following year. Jim Hutton lodged with friends until May, when he received his inheritance and purchased a house in Stamford Brook. He died of cancer on New Years Day 2010, three days before his 61st birthday.

Mary Austin still resides at Garden Lodge, which has been described as a cross between an impenetrable fortress and a mausoleum by the few outsiders who have had the privilege of entering its portals. For many years, little within the place was changed. 'M' told me in 1996, 'Freddie's bedroom is exactly the same now as it was the day he died. Not one item has been moved, and everything is covered in dust. It's sad to think of how he loved all these things in that room, or what he would think if he went back there now. One the eve of the Wembley tribute, Mary had given a rare interview to David Wigg. Admitting that five months after losing Freddie she was still unable to cry, she had confessed publicly exactly what those closest to him had known for years:

> Even in death I care about him and hope he's okay. I felt married to Freddie. It was for better or for worse. We had nothing when we met, so it was for richer or for poorer. And we stayed together when he was sick, so it was in sickness and in in health and until death us do part.

Soon after reading this moving testimony, Jim Hutton decided to 'put the record' straight', and with the help of a journalist named Tim Wapshott began compiling *Mercury & Me*, an account of his several years as Freddie's 'husband' –which was also his way of asserting his claims as the singer's 'widow'. John Dugdale of the *Sunday Times* labelled him 'the Sally Burton to Austin's Elizabeth Taylor' –referring to the well-publicised ill feeling between actor Richard Burton's widow and his former wife, to whom he had been married twice, a tempestuous union which for over a decade had resulted in them being the most talked about showbusiness couple in the world.

The result was a highly readable book with a pleasing mixture of pathos and camp, though cynics, susceptible third parties and, most importantly, several of Freddie's friends have questioned some of Hutton's more over-the-top anecdotes. One said, 'I'm surprised Jimmy could have stayed sober long enough to have remembered some of those things he did with Freddie.' Similarly, Mike Moran added, 'Jimmy used to get drunk and embarrass everybody and that's why he was never present at a lot of things he claimed to be.' Other friends have stated that Hutton's book might have been better received had it been co-written with one of Freddie's trusted journalist-allies, such as David Wigg. This almost certainly would have eliminated the over-use of words such as 'gay' and 'husband', wholly acceptable when used in their proper context, but overbearing when used as a sensationalist ploy in an attempt to sell books.

In fact, Wigg had been Hutton's first choice, as the journalist explained, 'I was going to do a book with Mary and she went cold on me at the last minute. And Jimmy *would* have done his book with me, if I hadn't promised to do Mary's. So in the end I lost out on both.' Even so, though Hutton had not actually put pen to paper, the dialogue and anecdotes—real or invented—were all his, recounted by a man who was entirely comfortable with his sexuality and unafraid of pulling out all the stops.

Mercury & Me contained much bad language. 'With Freddie, every other word began with F, but he always made cursing sound so hilarious!' Jacky Gunn recalled. There was much written about what had transpired in the bedroom, and much of the camp, ribald humour which had been an essential component of Freddie's personality, which might not have been welcomed by parents of younger, more impressionable fans. Freddie's father is alleged to have become physically ill after being read one anecdote, to which David Evans responded, 'They are going to find anything that's written about their son's "other business", as they called it, offensive because it's going to highlight the fact that he was homosexual, and that's what they cannot bear.'

Controversial, Jim Hutton's book may have been. It was also honest in its approach, bursting with compassion and respect for Freddie Mercury, the man, and just about every one of his surviving gay friends have maintained that he would have loved it. Hutton's importance, on the other hand, has been challenged by some, including Jim Jenkins, Queen's chronicler and official biographer who from his position on the group's periphery was able to draw a more plausible conclusion than most:

> Let's face it, Freddie and Jim did have a serious relationship, there's no question of that. But if Freddie loved Jim the way Jim says he did in his book, why didn't he leave him the house? If Jim really was his husband, then Freddie would have regarded him as his next of kin. If you're living in a house with somebody who's been your lover for six years, you don't leave it to a girlfriend from years ago, you leave it to the one you're with now. If Freddie was so much in love with him on his death-bed, why did he only leave him five-hundred grand? He also left Phoebe and Joe five-hundred grand, and they only worked for him. If I was his lover, I wouldn't be happy getting the same amount as somebody who was an employee.

Queen: As It Began, remains the definitive biography of the group, and appeared in 1992. The authors, Jacky Gunn and Jim Jenkins, had laboured painstakingly over the script for four years, most of the time wholly unaware that by the time of its completion, the house lights would be fading. Jenkins said, 'The script was ready for being edited in June 1991, then in the August we were told that it would have to be shelved until a later date. We weren't given an explanation, and I only found out two weeks before he died how really ill Freddie was.'

As the text had been completed at the time of Freddie's death, the authors decided not to jump on the sensationalist bandwagon by speculating exactly when Freddie had contracted AIDS. 'To have added such presumptions *after* his death would not have been fair,' Jacky said. 'Freddie had already read the script, and changing so much as a single sentence would have been us letting him down. He deserved better than that.'

On 26 May 1992, Queen's 1986 Wembley concert was released as a double album, completely unedited, and entered the charts at Number 2. On 16 November, to commemorate the first anniversary of Freddie's death the following week, EMI released *The Freddie Mercury Album*, a compilation of eleven of his solo songs—mostly reworked and remixed tracks from the by now deleted *Mr Bad Guy*, except for 'Time', 'In My Defence', and 'The Great Pretender.

Many fans disliked the album because, at just 44 minutes, it was way too short—and also because too many of the songs had been doctored. Roger Taylor denounced it in Queen's fan club magazine: 'I wish to point out that due to certain factors (solo projects) none of the three remaining members of Queen have been involved in any way with the record.' Even so, it was a fine tribute to a great artist, a little long in coming perhaps, and it reached Number 14 in the charts, eventually earning Freddie a posthumous gold disc. That summer, 'Barcelona' had been re-released as the theme for the Olympic Games and had reached Number 2—Freddie had been scheduled to perform it at the opening ceremony with Montserrat Caballé.

In the Queen saga, just one vital chapter remained. After four years deliberation and wrangling, Freddie's last seven songs were taken from the archives, and the surviving members of the group summoned to the studio to add their music and backing vocals to the tape. Several earlier tracks supplied enough material to make an album and *Made In Heaven* was released at the end of 1995—

shooting straight to the top of the charts. It had been a heartbreaking task which had affected all three of them badly. Brian May observed afterwards:

> This last album is one of the most ridiculously painful experiences I've ever had. I've done it for this album because I thought it was very important to get those last pieces of Freddie out. If it hadn't been for that, I wouldn't have wanted to do it. I valued my life more than the process.

The sleeve for *Made In Heaven* and it's two subsequent singles, 'Heaven For Everyone' and 'A Winter's Tale', was designed by Richard Gray, and though perhaps unethical in the way it was assembled using several of Gray's photographs, it is nevertheless very moving. Brian May, Roger Taylor and John Deacon (photographed in England) stand silhouetted with their backs to the camera in the grounds of the Duck House, gazing across Lake Geneva, while to their right stands the statue of Freddie (snapped in a field near Gray's home) which had attracted a great deal of attention in the months after his death, but which had yet to be assigned a suitable site. It was close to this tranquil spot that Freddie's ashes had been scattered.

With Freddie gone, and John Deacon retired from the group in 1997, Queen no longer exist as a working ensemble, and unless further archive material with Freddie is found and released, they will live on only in our memories and our hearts. Shortly after Freddie's death, Brian May declared, 'My personal feeling is that we should never go out and try and be Queen again. It doesn't make sense without Freddie.' Yet at the end of 2004, he and Roger Taylor recruited Middlesbrough-born Paul Rodgers, the 54-year old former frontman with Free and Bad Company. The following year, Queen + Paul Rogers embarked on a world tour, and in 2008 released a studio album, *The Cosmos Rocks*. Three live albums and several singles followed, and the outfit enjoyed a more than modest amount of success before splitting in 2009. Paul Rodgers was a competent singer—but he was not Freddie Mercury.

Of Freddie's unreleased work with Montserrat Caballé, there are six songs which can only be made commercially available with her consent, not Queen's. One is a rehearsal of them singing 'Music Of The Night' from Andrew Lloyd Webber's *Phantom Of The Opera*. Montserrat told me, 'Most of these pieces were taped at Freddie's home, and some never got as far as being given titles. There were two pieces that we really liked, and these were recorded in the studio, but we never got around to editing them, so I will never give permission for them to be released.' Michael Jackson's estate similarly owns the copyright to the two tapes he completed with Freddie—'Victory' and 'State Of Shock'. Freddie's tape-recordings of 'We Are The Champions' and 'Bohemian Rhapsody', were several couplets sung phonetically in Japanese, may also never see the light of day.

Freddie built his life on shifting sands, but his sublime showmanship and tragically early death have ensured him a place in legend, comparable only to the likes of Presley, Piaf, Valentino and Dean, and a mere handful of others. 'Queen without Freddie Mercury?' the journalist Tony Parsons once mused, 'Like *Casablanca* without Bogart, Morecambe without Wise? Toad without the hole?'

'Queen will never be an icon, but Freddie *always* will,' David Evans said, and he was of course absolutely right. Freddie remains completely irreplaceable.

(Redferns)

Lightning Source UK Ltd.
Milton Keynes UK
UKOW05f2212150714

235181UK00002B/254/P